AN
ENTREPRENEUR'S
GUIDE TO
FREEDOM

Seven Steps to Living Beyond Limits

MARK RAMPOLLA

Founder, ZICO Coconut Water & Co-Founder, GroundForce Capital

AN INC.
ORIGINAL

An Inc. Original
New York, New York
www.anincoriginal.com

Distributed by Greenleaf Book Group

For ordering information or special discounts for bulk purchases, please contact Greenleaf Book Group at PO Box 91869, Austin, TX 78709, 512.891.6100.

Design and composition by Greenleaf Book Group and Kimberly Lance
Cover design by Greenleaf Book Group and John van der Woude

Publisher's Cataloging-in-Publication data is available.

Print ISBN: 978-1-63909-064-8

eBook ISBN: 978-1-63909-065-5

To offset the number of trees consumed in the printing of our books, Greenleaf donates a portion of the proceeds from each printing to the Arbor Day Foundation. Greenleaf Book Group has replaced over 50,000 trees since 2007.

Printed in the United States of America on acid-free paper

25 26 27 28 29 30 31 32   10 9 8 7 6 5 4 3 2 1

First Edition

To Ciara and Lexi.
May you be safe.
May you be well.
May you be peaceful.
May you be free.

CONTENTS

IN SEARCH OF FREEDOM

It was a crisp Monday morning in the fall of 2017. After my workout, I walked down to what we called the Rancho—a rustic retreat we'd built on the edge of our oceanfront property in Redondo Beach, California. Five years earlier, my wife, Maura, and I had jumped at the chance to buy this property, lured by the real estate ad's promise: "Nothing between you and Hawaii." We had been living lean for nearly a decade, clinging to the dream that someday we'd be able to afford a place like this. After selling ZICO to The Coca-Cola Company in 2013, it was time to start cashing in on that dream and others. Over the next two years, we transformed the 1960s split-level house into a modern sanctuary. The Rancho was the final touch—a nod to the Latin America we loved. It sat perched above the Pacific, 250 feet below. Wide open. Limitless. Free.

It was still dark, just before 6 a.m.—my favorite time of day, when it felt like I had the world to myself. Our dog, Titus, settled at my side like he was gearing up for his own meditation practice—though his usually involved snoring and occasionally chasing dream squirrels. I closed my eyes, calmed my breathe, and went inward; something I'd done almost daily for over twenty years.

It started as a hobby in the Peace Corps, when I had time to spare. Later, during the chaos of building ZICO, it became a key tool in my entrepreneur's survival kit. For a year or two after selling ZICO in 2013, I meditated like a monk with nothing left to prove. Then life reminded me—I still had a lot to learn. That morning, mediation felt like a lifeline: applying duct tape to hold my sanity together.

The Pacific stretched out endlessly, peaceful and unbroken. But inside, I was anything but calm.

My mind raced. On the surface, the investment firm I cofounded, PowerPlant Ventures, looked like a home run, with investments in Beyond Meat and Thrive Market. But not so underneath. One of the companies we invested in, Juicero, was imploding. Several other companies were struggling. My personal finances? Let's just say I'd lost count of how many investments I had out there—and most were not looking good. Maura and I were navigating the toughest time yet in our marriage. My back ached, a reminder of the thousands of cases of ZICO I had loaded and unloaded for event sampling in the early years, and I hadn't been sleeping well. Tequila the night before didn't help.

I tried to let the thoughts pass like clouds in the sky, as I had trained myself to do. But they didn't. They swirled, circled, and grew darker by the minute.

Then, out of nowhere, came the question that stopped me cold: *Am I free?*

I sat with it. *Am I free?* I didn't know how to answer.

I thought back to moments when I had felt free: paddleboarding from the beach below our house to the nearby cove to catch wave after wave, playing freeze dance with the girls when they were little, hiking, skiing, gardening, lugging a piece of driftwood up the hill to turn it into art. Turning down a big promotion and quitting my corporate job to start ZICO—that felt like freedom. But the grind that followed? Nope. Racing to sell ZICO to Coca-Cola? Not so much.

I let the question hang there, and others followed. *If I were truly free, what would I do right now? Today? Would I be living this life?*

I laughed at the absurdity of the question. What would I do if I was totally free? Paddleboard all day? Garden? Start a new business? Teach a college course? Take off a year and backpack through Asia? Move to a monastery and finally figure out how to sit cross-legged without losing circulation? The truth was that I didn't know. What I did know was that I had a packed schedule, a mile-long to-do list, a tightness in my chest that had nothing to do with my workout that morning, a dog that wouldn't walk himself, and a mysterious sticky note I left for myself on my mirror that just said "URGENT."

But I also knew this: Despite achieving what I had once dreamed of—building ZICO, selling to Coca-Cola, millions in the bank, a small dose of fame, the beachfront home overlooking the Pacific—I didn't feel free.

And I couldn't shake the feeling that I had missed something important along the way. Something big.

That morning, I didn't find the answer. But I knew the question wasn't going away.

The ZICO Dream

In starting ZICO, I had a dream—one that looked a lot like the scene that morning in the Rancho. I imagined sitting in a beautiful home, gazing out at an amazing view, happily married, money in the bank, healthy and fit, a sense of satisfaction and accomplishment, free to do whatever I wanted, whenever I wanted. The reality, as I was starting to realize, felt quite different.

My journey with ZICO began in the early 1990s as a Peace Corps volunteer in Costa Rica. One scorching afternoon, dehydrated and dizzy, I gratefully took a coconut handed to me by a local. I sipped the strange but tasty liquid inside, and it worked like magic. A few years later, during a summer internship in Mexico, I passed out from dehydration. When I woke up in a hospital bed, there was no IV—just a lovely nurse handing me a coconut.

After grad school, Maura and I moved around with my corporate job at International Paper—first Memphis, then El Salvador—where coconut water was everywhere: We had pitchers of it in the fridge, mixed it into cocktails, used it post workout and as a hangover cure. It was part of daily life. As much as I liked my corporate job and was told my future was bright with the company, I couldn't shake the feeling that there was something more out there for me.

Maura saw it too. At an industry conference, during a mind-numbing presentation about "innovations in the dairy industry," she locked eyes with me from across the table and mouthed, "Get out."

I mouthed back, "Of the conference or the industry?"

She didn't blink. "Both."

After five years in El Salvador—and one too many dairy conferences—we both knew it was time for a change.

Slowly, coconut water transformed in my mind—from a drink to an idea and then an obsession. The late 1990s and early 2000s saw a boom in health-conscious beverage brands such as Vitamin Water, Honest Tea, and Hint. At the same time, I learned how the amazingly replenishing water inside coconuts, grown in over eighty-five tropical countries, was mostly discarded in the production of coconut milk, cream, and oil. The opportunity seemed clear: Create a modern and cool coconut water brand rooted in health, wellness and sustainability. If we got that right, we might even create an entire new category in the industry that would spur billions of dollars of investment across the tropical world and create thousands of jobs.

The dream was bold but simple: Build ZICO into a $100 million business, sell it to Coca-Cola, and leave them to scale it into a billion-dollar global brand. Then I'd be free—wealthy, successful, and in control of my time and life. I'd finally have the freedom to do whatever I wanted for the rest of my life.

In 2004, I raised $1 million from friends, family, and business associates in Central America and quit my corporate job, and we moved to New York with our two daughters to make it happen. I was excited. Energized. And most importantly, I felt free.

Starting and building ZICO was exhilarating—and then it was brutal.

Before I even quit my job, I worked nights, weekends, and vacations: researching beverage success stories like Red Bull and Snapple; studying cases of other companies that had built categories; creating a business plan; learning about coconuts in painstaking detail; figuring out how to source those with the best electrolyte profile and package the water without the typically used additives or preservatives; designing packaging, branding, and messaging; and learning all I could about how the US beverage market worked. We launched at the New York Fancy Food Show in the summer of 2004 with a lot of buzz and quickly landed Fairway Market, one of the top retailers in New York.

Hot yoga was booming at the time, and ZICO's hydrating properties made it a perfect post-workout drink. I hired a small team, and we hustled to get ZICO into every yoga studio in New York and every natural food store, deli, and bodega around them. We had purpose, passion, a strategy, and momentum.

But growth wasn't fast enough. Some months, we had more in parking tickets than sales. A paperwork glitch with the FDA forced us off shelves for nearly three months. The $1 million we raised vanished in six. I downsized the team and moved ZICO's headquarters into the loft above our garage—a space I had built (illegally and poorly) by hand.

Maura—who co-founded ZICO with me and early on wore numerous hats from public relations to morale booster (mainly mine)—eventually decided to step outside the company to find work that actually paid. It was the kind of move that likely saved our finances and marriage. Our relationship had flourished in El Salvador—one of the world's most dangerous places—but it turned out running a start-up together in a makeshift garage office was far more hazardous, especially after she decided my management style wasn't exactly "inspirational" and opted to lead herself right back into public health. We both braced ourselves for the realities of start-up life.

For five years, I hustled nonstop—up at 4:30 a.m. to schmooze distributors in the Big Geyser network, afternoons selling door-to-door in Manhattan, evenings packing boxes in the garage. Weekends, I loaded up the company van with a couple hundred cases, barrels, and ice and went to triathlons and running events to hand out ZICO to thirsty participants. Maura and the girls sometimes joined me, turning sampling into a full-family affair: Maura charming the crowd, the girls double-fisting samples, and me pretending we looked like a thriving start-up instead of a mobile lemonade stand. My sleep was a disaster, but I told myself "real entrepreneurs" didn't need it anyway.

Even as ZICO grew, I felt the pressure mounting. I wasn't just responsible for my family's future; I carried the weight of my investors, employees, and suppliers. I told myself I had to keep pushing. Harder. Faster. No breaks. No excuses. Occasionally, I wondered if I'd made a big mistake and should try to get my old job back. But more often I'd just deny, avoid, or bury any of those thoughts or the feelings they stirred up. *Just put your head down and keep plowing forward*, I told myself.

I swung between the fear of failing and being exposed as a fraud and the fear of succeeding only to realize I might be a selfish, miserable rich guy who still didn't know what he wanted to be when he grew up.

I blamed others when things went wrong—my team, suppliers, even the weather—but I saved my sharpest criticism for myself. One minute, I was convinced I was too much—too positive, too intense, too ambitious; the next, I worried I wasn't enough—too slow, too small, too "Mr. Nice Guy."

So I became an emotional escape artist, stuffing guilt, shame, fear, and anger into the world's most crowded mental junk drawer and slamming it shut with a to-do list. If I just kept moving, I wouldn't have to face what was piling up inside.

Then Came the American Express Bill

It was late—too late to be staring at bills—but there I was, trying to figure out how we'd pay it. The bottom line was larger than the balance in our checking account. I stormed into the bedroom, where Maura was folding laundry after a long day of work herself.

"Maura, have you seen this bill? We're drowning here!"

She calmly took the bill, scanned it, and pointed to a line item.

"'Girl's shoes—$19.99.'" She looked up at me. "Mark, we're not living excessively here."

I started to argue, but she wasn't finished.

"You got us into this. Now you need to get us out."

Then, she went back to folding laundry while I stood there, Amex bill in hand, feeling like I'd just been hit by a coconut.

So I doubled down. More hours. More effort. More pressure. I felt like I just had to do it alone.

The Breakthrough—or So I Thought

Despite the chaos, ZICO started to catch fire. There was no magic moment. It took a thousand little acts and countless hours from our relentlessly dedicated team and the distributors, retailers, and partners that believed in ZICO. By 2008, we had landed deals with Amazon, Whole Foods, and Trader Joe's. By 2009, ZICO was everywhere in New York and became one of the fastest growing beverages in the country. The mighty Coca Cola Company even took notice. After paying $4.1 billion for Vitamin Water in 2007, they seemed determined not to miss the next big one. They formed a new group, Ventures and Emerging Brands (VEB), to get in earlier with promising brands. In 2009, the VEB team approached me about investing in ZICO and asked if I'd be open to having Jesse Itzler, founder of Marquis Jet, invest and bring along a group of celebrities and athletes. I had met Jesse before—I knew he genuinely loved ZICO and had an insanely powerful network. What I didn't know until that moment was that he was also in discussions with Coca-Cola to start his own coconut water brand! I was thrilled to have Jesse on my team rather than as a competitor. I knew I needed all the help I could get—and I also knew that the celebrity/influencer world was definitely not my zone of genius. Now, with a big infusion of capital and the buzz and excitement Jesse and crew brought, ZICO started to really take off. In 2011, Coca-Cola bought more of the company, and in 2013, they bought ZICO outright for over $200 million.

Nine and a half years after launch, the dream became reality.

I had built the business, made the money, and achieved what I set out to do. *Now*, I thought, *it is time to slow down, reconnect with myself and my family, and finally—finally—be free.*

Or so I thought . . .

The first few months after the sale felt like a dream. My calendar was suddenly empty. I slept in, paddleboarded, took my daughters to school, and had long, wine-fueled lunches with Maura, where we actually finished sentences.

We traveled—Europe, Africa, Asia—and hosted friends and family at our new home. I tried my hand at a vegetable garden until everything died and I realized succulents were more my speed. It felt suspiciously like early retirement.

But not for long.

Entrepreneurs started coming to me—for advice, capital, and free lunches. I felt important and liked that. I started investing—writing five- and six-figure checks into dozens of businesses, like I was playing start-up bingo. We donated to nonprofits, and I joined a few boards. I wrote and published my first book, *High-Hanging Fruit*, and cofounded PowerPlant Ventures. I spoke at conferences and attended cool-kid events like Summit at Sea. I told myself I was paying it back and making an impact but now as a chilled, relaxed, post-success founder.

The truth? I was as busy as ever, maybe busier. PowerPlant alone was a bear: Figuring out how to raise, manage, and invest a venture capital fund alone was intense. I now had numerous personal investments to manage. I took on more and more personal, non-profit, and house projects. Vacations and parties got bigger and now required prep and recovery days. More travel. More deals. More everything. I was going like I was living out my final days before a long prison sentence.

Even with a big success under my belt, money in the bank, and the view of the Pacific from our Rancho, I found myself sitting there asking, *Am I free?*

I had spent years dreaming of freedom, only to realize I didn't really know what it looked or felt like—or if I'd ever truly have it.

Facing Reality

Four years after selling ZICO, as I meditated in the Rancho that fall morning, the truth hit me: I wasn't free.

I started taking inventory, assessing how free I felt in the areas where I hoped to be thriving.

Health: I was in good shape and generally healthy, but my back gave out every few months. If I wasn't in pain recovering, I was in fear of the next injury. Running? Basketball? Mountain biking? Three things I had loved for years—forget about it. I just didn't feel like I could do any of them without risking being out of commission for days or weeks.

Wealth: We had more money—even after buying and rebuilding our home—than I originally dreamed of. Enough that I never had to work again, as long as we didn't live too large. But somehow, what would have felt excessive just a few years earlier now felt . . . well, normal. And not enough.

So, I started investing aggressively and quickly wound up with a wild patchwork of more than 50—maybe 60—angel investments. I lost track. Every spring, the K-1s—those charming little tax forms that LLCs send to investors—began arriving like confetti from an exploding file cabinet. Gathering them became an annual ritual, somewhere between a scavenger hunt and a federal indictment.

I even fired my wealth manager—convinced I could handle it myself. After all, how hard could it be? I'd built and sold a company!

Just a few years earlier, I had tracked every dollar I spent. Now, I barely skimmed credit card bills. I didn't want to face the reality that some months, we spent more than my dad had made and raised six kids on in a good year.

I thought about the athletes and musicians who built fortunes only to watch them disappear. Was I really so different? Maybe keeping wealth is just as hard—even harder—than making it.

Habits: Wine at lunch? Why not. Champagne brunches? Of course. Expensive tequila "for special occasions"—which seemed to include Wednesdays? Newly legal cannabis? That's just *California sober*. It all felt like well-earned fun—at least until I started wondering if I was enjoying life or just numbing it.

Relationships: Maura and I weren't where we wanted to be. We fought more and couldn't seem to connect like we used to. We did everything we knew how to do to come back together—to reconnect, to rebuild, to create something new—but nothing seemed to work and we were both unsure what to do about it.. I had invited friends and family to follow me into various investments that proved to be anything but "sure things," straining many of those relationships. Professionally, I had plenty of contacts but not enough real connections. Lots of meetings but few with meaning.

I thought back on my ZICO journey and realized that, from the beginning, I had been following a sort of unconscious "success formula":

Vision + Hard Work = Success = Wealth = Freedom

Sure, there were other variables: purpose, risk, team, mindset, focus, persistence, and a dash of luck. But at its core, the formula was simple:

Dream big. Hustle hard. Cash out. Live free.

I had followed the formula to the letter. And I'd "made it." I was one of the winners.

Yet there I was, sitting in the Rancho, staring out at the Pacific—ocean view, dream house, money in the bank and all—still asking myself the same question: *Am I free? Or am I in a self-created prison with a killer view?*

That question lingered. It refused to go away.

And that morning, in the Rancho, I decided something had to change.

The Search for True Freedom

For the next five years, I led a double life. By day, I went about my normal routine as investor, board member, and firm partner. By nights, early mornings, weekends, and vacations, I became a full-time student of psychology, neuroscience, spirituality, and history.

I worked with leading therapists, coaches, spiritual guides, and shamans. I journaled, hiked, meditated, fasted, and did vision quests, plant medicine, holotropic breathwork, and more. I screamed, laughed, and wept. I dug deep—into my past and family, facing fears, peeling back layers of identity, and questioning the stories I'd heard, believed, and been telling myself for years, including the one that someday, I'd have it all figured out.

Maura and I did couples counseling—a painful but revealing process. We began to confront the cracks we'd both been papering over, and despite sharing the fantasy that our marriage would go the distance, we started to see the possibility that we might be better off separating, an ending neither of us had ever imagined.

What I uncovered through all of this work surprised me. Beneath all the striving and achievements, I saw how much I had been living according to "shoulds" and "shouldn'ts"—other people's expectations, not my own. In many ways, I was deeply unsure and conflicted about what I wanted, and the result was I wasn't living *my* life. I was like a dog in the woods, darting after every squirrel-shaped version of success that crossed my path, never stopping long enough to ask if I even liked squirrels in the first place.

And I wasn't alone.

I saw it—and heard about it—again and again from countless entrepreneurs I met in boardrooms, coffee shops, events, and parties. Some appeared to have it all: exits bigger than mine, private jets, sprawling estates, and businesses worth millions or billions. Yet they didn't feel free. They were restless, anxious, and exhausted—still chasing "just a little more." Others who didn't win big seemed stuck in perpetual survival mode—too broke to scale, too proud to quit—like contestants on *Survivor* who refused to tap out even after eating bugs and losing twenty pounds. Some were trapped in cycles of denial, shame, and endless makeovers, trying to figure out who they were, what they stood for, and what to say about themselves on their LinkedIn profiles.

I started to more openly share my own struggles with fellow entrepreneurs—how, when faced with the brutal reality of startup life, I tried to cut off my emotions, thinking feelings were a liability, terrified that if I let myself feel fear, it would spiral into paralysis and failure, and I'd often hear sheepishly, "Thank you for sharing that. I thought I was the only one."

Whether we had made it big or were still deep in the mud and weeds, we were like swans gliding effortlessly on the surface, but underneath, we were paddling furiously, trying not to sink.

The more I listened, the clearer it became: Most of us—no matter how much success, wealth, or fame we had—weren't free.

And that's when I wondered if the formula we had all bought into was fundamentally flawed.

Hacking the Formula

I started to dissect and tear apart this formula that I had in my head:

Vision + Hard Work = Success = Wealth = Freedom

It worked—for a while. Until it didn't.

I realized how deeply I'd bought into delayed gratification—the belief that freedom is always "over there," just one more deal or milestone away. It's a mindset embedded in entrepreneurial culture: Hustle now, be free later.

But later never came.

There's power in delayed gratification, but I began to wonder if that was the only or always the best approach.

The first challenge I recognized is that no matter how detailed the formula, the odds are overwhelmingly against entrepreneurs. A staggering 90 percent of start-ups fail, and about 10 percent don't even make it past the first year.[1] That's right: By the time you're printing your first branded hoodies, they might become collector items.

For the brave souls who stick it out, the odds don't exactly improve. Only about 0.4 percent of tech companies ever reach $10 million in annual recurring revenue, and it's certainly no better in other industries.[2]

And personal wealth? Despite the dream of creating generational wealth, passive income, and working from the beach, the average entrepreneur in the US made just $95,575 in 2024,[3] slightly more than the median US household income of $81,000.[4]

---

1 Alla Adam, "90% of Startups Fail—How to Secure Your Place in the 10%." Forbes, September 10, 2024. https://www.forbes.com/councils/forbescoachescouncil/2024/09/10/90-of-startups-fail how-to-secure-your-place-in-the-10/.

2 Tomasz Tunguz, "SAAS Success Metrics," Venture Capitalist at Redpoint Ventures, https://tomtunguz.com/saas-success-metrics.

3 "Top Executives," Occupational Outlook Handbook, US Bureau of Labor Statistics, https://www.bls.gov/ooh/management/top-executives.htm, and Payscale/Indeed https://www.payscale.com/research/US/Job=Entrepreneur/Salary.

4 "HINC-01. Selected Characteristics of Households by Total Money Income," US Census Bureau, 2024, https://www.census.gov/data/tables/time-series/demo/income-poverty/cps-hinc/hinc-01.html.

As for the elusive big payday? Well, only about 1 percent of start-ups ever raise a Series D funding round, at which point founders are still hoping for a big IPO.[5]

And from my own experience—along with conversations with hundreds of entrepreneurs—I've seen firsthand that very few ever achieve a level of success they find truly satisfying.

Previous success helps—a little. It improves the odds of success from 10 percent to 30 percent,[6] but let's be honest: That's hardly a guarantee. So the first part of the formula? Questionable at best.

The second flaw in the formula became painfully clear—not just for me, but for so many others. Even if the formula works, even if you achieve the success and wealth you dream of, there's still no guarantee of freedom. Whether it's $1 million or $1 billion, no amount of money fixes what's unresolved inside.

Entrepreneurs are optimists. We're confident. We believe we're different, and in many ways, we are. We tell ourselves that our story will be different—it has to be. Because we believe. Because we work so hard. Maybe it will be. Maybe not.

But just like we can't escape gravity, we can't escape reality.

That's when I began to wonder, *What if there was a different way? What would happen if I flipped the formula?*

Instead of waiting to experience freedom when I "made it," could I have started with freedom from the beginning? Could I begin anew with freedom first—right here, right now?

I committed then and there: whatever the situation, I would face

---

5 "Venture Capital Funnel Shows Odds of Becoming a Unicorn Are About 1 Percent," CB Insights, September 6, 2018, https://www.cbinsights.com/research/venture-capital -funnel-2/.

6 Paul A. Gompers et al., "Performance Persistence in Entrepreneurship and Venture Capital," *Journal of Financial Economics* 96, no. 1 (April 2010): 18–32.

reality head-on, experience it fully, and do my best not to compromise my freedom.

Part of that reality was this tension: I wanted to feel like I had enough, that I was enough—but I also knew that part of me would never be satisfied. I wanted more. More success. More wealth. More love. More meaning. What if that desire wasn't something to be ashamed of but something to be celebrated as part of who I was and how I wanted to live?

What if freedom wasn't the reward at the end of the journey, but foundational for me to create the conditions for the success, wealth, love, and meaning I wanted?

So I began to test it out—making freedom my starting point.

Slowly, this shift changed everything.

Day by day, situation by situation, I got better at simply being present—experiencing life as it was, not as I thought it should be. I started by just observing the stories I was telling myself and the emotions they triggered. Then I began to question whether the stories were true or not and truly experience my emotions without numbing or avoiding them. For the first time, I got to know, accept, appreciate, and love myself in ways I never had before.

Sure, I overreacted sometimes. I triggered myself. I got emotional. But I realized it was all just part of being human. I learned to see it, accept it, and then shift back to a state of freedom.

I became more intentional—more choiceful—about where, how, and with whom I spent my time, energy, and attention. I learned to listen more, react less, and contain whatever was happening inside me, responding—if I chose to—with clarity, intention, and confidence.

I examined my habits and patterns, this time with curiosity instead of judgment, and I let go of many that no longer served me.

I still worked hard. I still had drive and ambition. In fact, I had even more of it, because I was finally in touch with that insatiable part of me that always wants more. But at the same time, I learned to relax, to observe, to get into the flow. I learned to hold my attachment to the outcome lightly—to surrender. To enjoy the ride. To allow space for something even greater than I had imagined.

My decisions became easier. My energy stronger, steadier, and more enduring. My relationships deeper.

I experienced more joy—not just in work, but in life.

And the results? They were undeniable.

I was getting more of what I wanted—personally, professionally, financially. And when I didn't, I could see it as just another experience, another lesson, another opportunity to learn.

I was so energized by what I was experiencing that I wanted to bring it into the investment firm I had cofounded and renamed GroundForce (more on that later). My business partner, Dan Gluck—a former hedge fund manager and intense athlete—was skeptical but intrigued. He had noticed how much more calm, focused, and intentional I had become. He wasn't exactly a "let's talk about our feelings" guy, but together with a team of world-class coaches, we began reimagining not just our lives but our business.

We transformed our boutique venture fund into an institutional investment firm—embedding the tools and techniques we were learning into our systems, strategies, and culture. It took our team a little while to adjust to meetings in which we asked them to "check in with their emotions" instead of just the balance sheets, but the impact was undeniable. We started making better decisions.

We haven't achieved everything we want yet. We both know, and can laugh at the fact, that we'll never be fully satisfied. But we're not waiting for freedom anymore.

We're living it.

And that's the point.

You don't have to wait. You don't have to hit a specific number, close a certain deal, or check off the next goal before you allow yourself to feel free.

You can be free now.

And this isn't just about freedom—it's about getting more of what you want from life. More success. More income. More wealth in all it's forms. More meaning. Deeper relationships. Whatever it may be.

Freedom isn't the finish line; it's the starting line.

Freedom isn't the prize; it's the power source.

It fuels bigger goals, bigger wins, and a bigger impact.

And, more than anything, it fuels a richer, more meaningful life.

A New Path Forward

This book isn't just about breaking free from the grind; it's about rewriting your own success formula and using freedom as fuel rather than the end goal.

I'll share my experiences—what worked, what didn't—and the tools, frameworks, and habits that helped me stop chasing and start living.

In seven steps, I'll show you how to

- Break free from autopilot and reclaim your time, energy, and focus

- Redefine success on your terms—not someone else's

- Let go of limiting beliefs and create a future bigger than you ever imagined

- Take bigger risks with confidence—because you're already free
- Live the life you want now—without waiting for "someday"
- Future-proof your freedom from uncertainty and disruptions such as war, economic instability, and technologies like AI

Each chapter includes a personal story, key insights, and practical tools you can apply immediately. Read it straight through, or pause and dive into the tools whenever you're ready.

Your freedom. Your journey. Your pace.

What This Book Is NOT

This isn't a step-by-step manual for building a business or striking it rich—there's no shortage of books, coaches, courses, and YouTube videos promising that. In my experience, and in conversations with countless entrepreneurs, those resources can be useful—but rarely enough to deliver lasting success or real wealth.

And when it comes to freedom? They fall flat.

Achieving enduring success, wealth in all it's forms (financial, health, relational), and true freedom demands something deeper—a stronger foundation.

That's where this book focuses: helping you ground yourself in freedom so you can build whatever you want.

Because freedom fuels success.

The Invitation

I know this may sound too good to be true. You might be skeptical.

Good.

Keep questioning. But notice it. Notice the doubts. Be aware of the skepticism. Freedom takes awareness. Awareness must be cultivated.

How will you know if what I share is true? Don't take my word for it. Check in with yourself along the way: Do you feel freer? Are you seeing better results? Are you getting more of what you want from your business, relationships, and life?

There is no substitute for your own direct experience.

Freedom cannot be taught. It is not conceptual. It cannot be "AI-ified." It must be experienced.

If you're curious, read on.

What's the worst that could happen? You might gain a new perspective. You might realize that freedom isn't something you have to wait for; it's something you already own.

And realizing that? It's delicious.

As one of my favorite coaches, Kat, says, it's like having your cake, eating it too, and staying thin forever.

So let's begin.

The journey toward—or back to—freedom starts now.

SEE AND ACCEPT REALITY: YOU ARE NOT AS FREE AS YOU THINK

Inside a nondescript building in Palos Verdes, a well-to-do hilly suburb of Los Angeles that juts out into the Pacific, my therapist, Agnes, welcomed me into her cozy room filled with sunlight, books, plants, and well-organized toys and games in one corner. I had been to therapy once in college, but that was more like splashing around in the kiddie pool. After three years working with Agnes, this was like scuba diving into the deep waters of my mind. I didn't know what I'd see or experience over the next ninety minutes, but I trusted that my skilled dive master would keep me safe and help me interpret the strange sights I might see. As I settled onto the familiar off-white couch with the burnt-orange cushions, she greeted me with a smile. "So, how are you, Mark?"

"Well, let's see . . ." I paused, practicing checking in with myself instead of giving the automatic "Great!" I might give in a typical business setting.

Finally, I said, "I feel both anger and sadness," carefully using the language she encouraged, even though it still felt a bit unnatural to me. "It's been another interesting week. 'Adventures in Capital,'

I like to call it. Can I just bitch and moan a little about work?" She smiled and invited me to go ahead. By that point I knew I could share anything without fear of judgment. By going deep into any experience, I learned something about myself applicable to almost every part of my life, whether I liked it or not.

I vented about work, frustrated that my partner, Dan, wouldn't back an investment I was convinced would be a winner. He pushed back, questioning whether we should focus on more mature companies instead of start-ups.

Agnes listened, then said, "Sounds like you really want to be right about this. Are you open to seeing it from his perspective?"

I paused. "Honestly? No. Maybe I should be. Maybe I will be. But not right now."

She nodded. "Good. I'm not saying you should or shouldn't. That's your choice. But at least you're being honest with yourself—that's just where you are at this moment."

I talked about how one of our portfolio companies had struggled.

"I just don't think the founder is facing reality. He didn't make cuts fast enough when growth slowed and they were running out of money.," I said. "We don't have more money ourselves to invest, and other investors won't fund money-losing businesses right now."

"So what happens next?" Agnes asked.

"Well, they may not survive. They may have to shut down or sell the company at a loss."

"And then what? Play it all the way out for me. What's the worst that can happen? Get dramatic!"

"Well, if the company fails, we lose all our money. We have a couple big winners in our fund, but it also looks like we have more failed investments than we expected, including two that I stepped in to run as interim CEO."

I became more and more animated. "And then the investors revolt, we get sued, and I end up living in my car—probably an old Volvo with a missing hubcap."

I slumped back. "I'm supposed to be this great manager who knows what he's doing, and look at my track record! I'm a terrible investor and a shitty CEO. I'm not sure I see a way out." I could feel heat rising to my head and my shoulders and my back tightening.

I groaned. "And the worst part? People will just shake their heads and say, 'Remember that ZICO guy? Man, he had it all. What a tragedy.' Like I'm some washed-up reality show contestant."

"Are you sure about all of that, Mark?" she asked. "You say the CEO isn't seeing reality, but are you certain you are?"

The question annoyed me—an almost certain sign of truth. That pissed me off even more. I was also disappointed in myself, realizing that the peace and calm I had felt just a few minutes ago had already vanished. She paused, as she so often does, and quietly yet firmly cautioned, "Mark, you're getting a little defensive. I'm not attacking you. I'm just trying to shed a little light on what you may not want or be able to see. Tell me if I'm wrong, but it appears to me you have a lot going on. You are pulled in so many directions."

"All right," I finally said, now laughing at myself. "I can see that." I took a slow, steady breath. I grunted a not-so-quiet "urgh" trying to release it all.

"How are you holding up personally? What's going on at home?"

I opened up about my physical health, the lack of sleep, the excruciating back pain that had flared recently, as it seemed to do every three months or so. I talked about my parents: my mom's failing health and moving her and my dad from Pittsburgh to be near us. I admitted to falling back into the habit of getting up earlier and earlier to "get shit done," drinking almost every day and more on weekends. It hit me: This felt like the early years of ZICO—only now with pricier wine and worse back pain. Back then, with every penny invested in the company and me taking a paltry salary, it seemed like we had no money. The stress for Maura and me was constant. We got through that, but it was a tough nine years. I thought the success of ZICO and the money we made selling the company would mean I would feel free. And yet here I was, feeling fearful and trapped again. I could see that though my bank account might have a few more zeros, the feelings of scarcity remained. Handcuffs are handcuffs, whether they are rusty iron or 24-karat gold.

I spoke about our youngest daughter going off to college and how Maura and I would be empty nesters. Maura had hoped we'd spend more time together after selling ZICO. She didn't seem to understand why I still worked long hours and was involved in so many businesses.

"She wants us to take a six-month vacation in Italy when Lexi leaves," I said. "When she suggested that, I nearly lost it: 'Did you miss the memo? We're hoping to launch our next fund, and I'm up to my ears helping our existing companies. I can't take a trip like that anytime soon. You should go, and I'll join for a couple weeks.' She was furious, then sad and disappointed—disappointed in me, I think, really."

"Why do you think that?"

I shifted in my seat and exhaled, feeling that same heaviness in my chest. "I don't like admitting this, but I do remember us talking about that trip years ago. It was a shared dream at the time. I think that dream helped her get through the darkest days of ZICO, when we could barely afford a dinner out, let alone a trip to Italy.

"I can see I'm disappointed in myself. My wife wants to spend time with me, and we can finally afford to take any trip we want, and I don't feel free to do so. How ridiculous is that?"

"Mark, I'm not saying anyone is right or wrong here, but can you take responsibility for how you cocreated this?" Agnes asked. "Can you see you're not accepting reality and seeing Maura and yourself exactly where and how you each are?"

That one stung. "I guess I can see that," I said, dragging out the words like they were being pried from my mouth. "But I'm definitely not happy about it."

Touching on my many commitments, Agnes quipped, "So clearly, you're getting pulled in all sorts of directions, but who exactly is driving the Mark bus? Is it you or everyone around you?"

Hearing the word *bus*, I said, "That reminds me of a dream I had last night."

Agnes, always excited to dive into dream analysis, said, "Great. I'd love to hear about that."

I closed my eyes and took a few slow, even breaths and started to recount.

"I'm driving a truck full of big wooden crates along a windy coastal road, somewhere foreign, maybe Italy. The Amalfi coast, I think. The road is narrow, steep, and winding, with a sheer drop to jagged rocks and the sea below. I'm struggling to turn the steering wheel. I try to downshift and brake, but neither helps. I can't control my speed. I try to open the door and get my feet on the ground to slow the truck while still steering. I feel like I have to be on time with the crates. I'm tired but can't stop because I'm afraid someone might steal or damage them, and I can't let that happen. That's when I wake up."

I paused for a moment, as if waking up from the dream again. "Fascinating," she said gently. "What's in the crates?"

I explained how each wooden crate was about four cubic feet, and there were ten or twelve of them in the truck. I don't know what was in them, but I knew they were fragile and important. I felt responsible for keeping them safe.

She asked where I was going with them.

I explained how I was heading toward a peaceful mountain town. Once I made it over the hills, I could cruise to my destination to rest and relax.

She asked what I felt in the dream.

I said the dominant feeling was fear. Fear of going off the road. Fear of losing or destroying what was in the crates and fear of disappointing the people who were waiting for them. They trusted me. I didn't feel like I had a choice. As I was driving, I could feel the crates moving around, and I was afraid they might break or fall out of the truck.

"What comes to your mind with this dream? Any associations?"

"I think the crates are the companies I'm involved with, and my family, my marriage, our girls, my parents. Each crate represents a responsibility, an obligation. This is my reality: I have all these responsibilities and sometimes feel I don't have full control over my life. It's like I'm playing Jenga, but instead of pulling out blocks, life just keeps stacking more on top and saying, 'You've got this!'"

"Mark, I think this dream is about a wish to have more control in your life, more freedom," she responded. "You're recklessly driving while dreaming about freedom and going so fast, you just can't allow yourself to slow down and be in control, even in your dreams, let alone in waking life. Your freedom is not Dan's or Maura's or your parents' or the CEO's responsibility. They've got their own things going on. Can you own that you are the creator, the driver of your own reality?"

She said she imagined I was doing my best in most situations—just as Dan, Maura, and the founders were. "Maybe you wish they were different. Maybe you wish reality were different. But right now, it's not."

She continued, "The first step to freedom is recognizing you're in a self-created prison. It doesn't matter how you got there, who's to blame, or if the door is even locked. See it, accept it, and own your role in it."

"I can see that," I said.

She continued, "The good news is you hold the key, and you've had it all along."

Accepting Reality Is the First Step Toward Freedom

That moment in my therapist's office on a random Friday crystallized something profound within me. Until then, I, like most entrepreneurs, thought of myself as free. I made bold moves like joining the Peace Corps, traveling the world, founding ZICO, and cofounding PowerPlant Ventures. I liked to consider myself the embodiment of freedom.

Looking back, I wasn't as free as I thought. I was unaware—or ignoring—so much of what was happening in my mind and body. I had a formula in my head for freedom: Dream big, work hard, build a successful business with impact. Sell it, make a fortune, gain some recognition. Voilà: success and freedom.

I followed this "formula" without really questioning it. I achieved what I set out for, even more by some measures, but I still did not feel free. What if ZICO had not worked out as I planned? Would I be chasing this dream of freedom forever?

Now it seemed like I was doing it all over again. I was waiting until some future state—when our companies exited, or I made the next chunk of money, or our firm grew to $1 billion in assets, or Mom regained her health, or my marriage was different—to feel free. Maybe I would achieve that, maybe not. What was I waiting for? I could see I wasn't taking responsibility for my situation and life. I was complaining about Dan, Maura, my parents, the founders—all of whom are smart, caring, important people in my life—and I'm blaming them for my thoughts and feelings. When I focused my attention on them, wanting them to change or be different, I wasn't present at all. I wasn't seeing and accepting reality. I was living in the past or future—anywhere except the here and now. It felt like I'd taken the blue pill in *The Matrix*—just coasting along, pretending everything was fine, eating my AI-generated, plant-based steak.

In that state of mind, I would then send myself into a frenzy. Like in my dream, going faster and faster, swerving out of control. Diving into "solve and get shit done" mode. I now see that in that mode, I was less capable of seeing possibilities, potential, and opportunities of all sorts. I wanted to be right, and those thoughts and stories and my inability to accept and process the feelings they stirred up in me held me back from enjoying and appreciating the present moment. I couldn't really choose freely what I wanted or how to respond.

Maybe I didn't really want to be free. Freedom sounds great, but I could see it would take work. It would be disruptive. It would be risky. Maybe ignorance really is bliss—like ignoring the "check engine" light and convincing yourself it's just a suggestion.

At that moment, I decided I did want to be free, and I was willing to do whatever it took. I realized reality itself wasn't the problem. Nothing was inherently wrong—not with me, Dan, Maura, my parents, the founders, or even the experiences I was having. The real issue was the stories I was telling myself—the blame, shame, "shoulds," and "shouldn'ts."

By resisting reality, wanting it to be different, I was creating my own pain and suffering—blinding myself to what was right in front of me, including countless opportunities to get what I wanted. Worse, I wasn't even taking steps to change what I could.

I was stuck.

I could see I was in a prison of my own creation—complete with imaginary bars, a warden who looked suspiciously like me, and zero chance of parole. At least seeing that, I could start to plot my great escape.

FREEDOM TOOL:
Locating Yourself: Right Now, Do You Feel Trapped, or Are You Free?

You may know the adage in real estate that "location, location, location" is the most critical factor in determining the value of a home. So, too, in freedom work, knowing where you are at any moment is the first and most important step. Most of us spend most of our time in a trapped state. It's completely normal. Acknowledging that is a critical step if we want to shift to a state of freedom. We'll talk later about how to shift to freedom, but for now, start by seeing where you are at any time. It's helpful to think about this as one or the other, either free or trapped, not somewhere in between. If you feel "sort of trapped," call it trapped. Do so with kindness and compassion—no shame, no blame, just reality. Here are some clues:

Are you free? How do you know? Use this guide to look at your thoughts, beliefs, statements, or questions to check in on your level of freedom.	
TRAPPED	**FREE**
Feeling defensive or reactive. "Why is this happening to me?"	Feeling open or curious. "How might this be happening for me?"
Thinking in terms of black-and-white and taking your thoughts and stories as fact without examining or questioning them.	Seeing the gray and examining, questioning, and challenging your thoughts. Is it true? Am I certain? What if the opposite were true?
Ignoring, denying, or avoiding emotions or numbing them with food, drugs, drink, sex, or media.	Feeling, identifying, and owning all the feelings. Where do I feel it in my body? What is it telling me? Sitting with your emotions.
Wanting to be right.	Willing to learn and grow.

Feeling shame and blame: for self, others, the world.	Taking 100% responsibility. Compassion for self and other.
Scarcity. Zero sum. Win–lose. "I don't have enough or what I want. Everyone in the world is against me. Nobody gets me."	Abundance. Appreciation. "I have enough. All I ever need is inside me now. Everyone and everything are for me." Seeking and seeing "wins for all."
Fighting reality: He/she/I/they "should"/"shouldn't"/"can't"/"must."	Accepting reality: I guess this is just happening. Now what do I want?
Everything takes effort, is a struggle, or is serious.	Any situation can be approached with ease, fun, lightness, and playfulness.
No choice. No option. Only "this" or "that": right/wrong, good/bad, always/never, black/white.	Choice. Possibilities. Creation. Many options. Ideas from anywhere, anyone. Knowing there are many options, outcomes.
Not listening. Not hearing others: "Why would you say that?" "What's wrong with you?" "Don't make me feel that way!" "You shouldn't feel that way!"	Active, engaged listening: "What I hear you saying is . . ." "I appreciate you sharing . . ." "I can own that." "I feel . . ."
Feeling the need to explain or justify what or why you do, say, act, or don't act	Respectfully and honestly owning what you want, do, and say and communicating that as you choose.
Protecting, deflecting, denying, or "returning fire" when you feel under threat.	Willing to be vulnerable and own your feelings and reactions.
Body feels: Stiff. Tight. Barely mobile. Holding back and feeling like you might explode. Holding your breath.	Body feels: Loose. Relaxed. You can and do move, shift, shake. Release. Breathing easily.
Unknowingly seeking external satisfaction for core desires of acknowledgment, control, security, and happiness.	Owning and asking for or being your own source for acknowledgment, control, security, and happiness.
Being intolerant. Being the enforcer: "You said you would!" "Why do you always . . ." "Why don't you ever . . ."	Being tolerant: Giving yourself and others a break, benefit of the doubt, and space to be human.

Example:

Let's use the story I mentioned about Dan and me as an example. If I was feeling **trapped**, I might think, *Why is this happening to me? Why doesn't Dan trust my judgment? Why do I always have to fight to prove my ideas? This is so unfair: I'm trying to do what's best, and he's just blocking me! He just doesn't get me!* From that place, I'd probably feel defensive, frustrated, and stuck—like I had no choice but to push harder or give up entirely.

But if I was feeling **free**, I might be able to ask, *I wonder how this is happening for me? Maybe Dan's right. Maybe his resistance is giving me a chance to clarify my thinking and make an even stronger case. Maybe I have a blind spot and there's something I'm missing. Maybe this is an opportunity to build more trust and collaboration in our partnership.* From that mindset, I am curious, creative, and open to possibilities—turning what felt like an obstacle into a chance to find the best solution and to grow and strengthen our partnership.

The Takeaways
Step 1: See and Accept Reality. You're Not as Free as You Think

What's the Point?

Success and freedom both require seeing and accepting reality. Part of that reality is that we're often not as free as we think. The path to freedom begins by recognizing and accepting that.

Why Is This Important?

We often trap ourselves in patterns of defensiveness, blame, and rigid thinking. Recognizing these mental and emotional traps and how we try to avoid, deny, or ignore them is the first step toward liberation. *Ignorance may feel like bliss, but it's ultimately the death of freedom and success.*

How To: Better See Reality

- **Use** the Trapped or Free guide.

- **Get curious:** Instead of *Why is this happening to me?* ask, *How might this be happening for me?* This shift opens curiosity and possibilities.

- **Notice patterns without judgment:** Observe your behaviors, emotions, and the stories you tell yourself. Simply noticing these habits without shame helps loosen their grip.

Go Deeper

- **Books:**

  - *Loving What Is* by Byron Katie
  - *Radical Acceptance* by Tara Brach
  - *The Obstacle Is the Way* by Ryan Holiday

- **Tools (markrampolla.co):**

  - The Drama Triangle
  - The Fact-Check Method
  - Taking 100% Responsibility

What's Next?

Now that we've identified what keeps us stuck, we'll explore how to shift to freedom—and it starts with the most important relationship you have in this life: the one with yourself. In Step 2, we'll dive into how knowing, owning, and celebrating yourself creates a foundation for lasting freedom and success.

KNOW, OWN, AND CELEBRATE YOURSELF

I woke up early on Saturday morning and looked out over the vast Pacific Ocean, the sun still hidden behind the hills, my family sound asleep. I had promised myself a long hike, and I was eager to follow through. The trails of Pacific Palisades felt like the perfect place for some much-needed mobile introspection. Living by the beach had its perks, but I craved the hills—the trees, the quiet that was different from the sound of crashing waves. Our dog, Titus, seemed to sense my excitement. He did a lazy downward dog stretch before bounding out of his little bed and following me into the bathroom, ready for adventure.

I dressed quickly, grabbed Titus's leash, a liter of ZICO, my backpack, and a long-sleeve shirt, and we were out the door. The 405 freeway would have been the quickest route to the Palisades, but I opted for the Pacific Coast Highway instead. As the road twisted away from the coastline, I wound my way through the hills, turned onto Sunset Boulevard and then Mandeville Canyon Road, continuing higher until I reached the small dirt parking lot at Westridge Trailhead.

It was just after 6 a.m., and the air was cool and damp with fog, adding a sense of mystery to the morning. Titus leaped from the car, his energy infectious. I snapped on his leash and threw the ZICO in my backpack, and we set off. As we walked, my mind wandered back to the conversation I'd had with my therapist the day before. She had nudged me to reflect on a hard truth: I wasn't as free as I had believed.

That realization stung. After all, wasn't freedom one of the main reasons I had left a good paying corporate job to pursue entrepreneurship in the first place? There are many types of freedom—financial freedom, creative freedom, time freedom—but I began to question whether, despite my success, I was truly experiencing any of them. The truth was, I wasn't. I was just living a different kind of trap—still on a hamster wheel but with nicer office furniture and fancier coffee.

An old business adage popped into my mind: "Whoever sees reality wins." It's something I had always believed, especially as an entrepreneur. If you don't see what's really happening—whether it's with your customers, your competition, or your own team—you'll lose. But it occurred to me that this principle didn't just apply externally; it was also true on the inside. I began to see how my internal world—my thoughts, emotions, desires, and the stories I told myself—was just as important and influential as what was happening around me, if not more so.

I realized I had been avoiding my emotions, dismissing them as irrelevant or even as weaknesses. But what if they were simply part of my reality, like everything else? What if my emotions were less like roadblocks and more like a built-in GPS—sometimes annoying, often dramatic, but ultimately trying to help me avoid driving off a cliff?

As Titus and I climbed higher along the trail, I thought about other entrepreneurs I knew—people who, from the outside, seemed wildly successful and free. Yet beneath the surface, I had come to see that many were trapped by their own ambitions, always striving but never stopping to reflect, recharge, integrate their learnings, or celebrate their accomplishments. They seemed like they were burdened by the weight of expectations—both their own and others'.

Was I any different? I could see now how I had fallen into that same trap, constantly pushing myself, trying to live up to an ideal that didn't really belong to me. I had been striving to be some "perfect" entrepreneur, chasing an image of success shaped by outside influences—what I read, what I saw, what I thought I should be. But did that really work in entrepreneurship? Did it work in life? Was that freedom?

That recent conversation with my therapist came to mind. She had pointed out my tendency to take on too much, to keep adding new projects without considering the toll it took on my health and relationships. I recognized the truth in her words and knew I still had so much to learn about myself.

As I continued hiking, I began to reflect on what I had learned about myself over the years. I had had many conversations with my therapist and coaches, taken personality tests, and sought feedback from my team, from Dan, and from others. Slowly, I began to piece together a clearer picture of who I was—what I valued, what motivated me, how I appeared to others, and what really mattered to me and what didn't.

What I valued most were creativity, exploration, the satisfaction of getting things done, and the freedom to pursue a goal, change my mind, and mix up my day, week, month, and year. Security, on the other hand, wasn't high on my list. I liked making money, sure, and I wanted more, but it wasn't for the financial safety it would provide. I thought back to my time as a Peace Corps volunteer, living on $187 a month. I sure didn't want to go back to that, but I realized that I didn't feel insecure then and I didn't now. Security wasn't what drove me. Routine didn't matter to me either—in fact, I actively disliked it. I thrived on variety, the freedom to pivot and try new things.

What did I need to be at my best? I had to laugh at how long I had convinced myself that I didn't have needs—they were a sign of weakness. But of course I did. We all do. I needed time alone to recharge. Turns out, I wasn't always the strong, tireless lone wolf; sometimes, I wanted to be more like Titus, curled up on the couch, pretending to be independent but secretly hoping someone would scratch behind my ears and tell me everything's going to be OK.

I thought about the blind spots I had uncovered over the years. I was great at spotting opportunities but sometimes too eager to jump without a parachute. Dan was the opposite—bringing discipline to my crazy ideas and diligence to my intuition. If I was the gas pedal, Dan was the brake—and together, we made sure the car moved ahead but didn't end up in a ditch.

This wasn't just surface-level self-awareness anymore. Therapy had helped me go deeper—to name these patterns, see where they showed up, and understand them. I felt like I was waking up in a whole new way. It wasn't about fixing myself; it was about meeting myself—with honesty, curiosity, compassion, a little humor, and—dare I say it in a business book—love.

Coaching, on the other hand, had been like gathering tools, and now I was finally starting to build something real with them. I was learning to catch myself in the act—those moments when I defaulted to fixing, overcommitting, or running on adrenaline. And instead of shaming myself for it, I could pause, notice, laugh, and choose my next step more consciously.

As I hiked on, I realized how much I had been holding myself to some unrealistic standard. I constantly criticized myself, trying to "fix" everything I saw as a flaw. But what if, instead of criticizing, I could celebrate these traits? What if I could surround myself with people who appreciated my strengths and complemented my weaknesses? What if I could finally own who I was—completely—and celebrate it, love it, warts and all?

That's what I wanted—what I think we all want. To wake up to ourselves. To be seen, heard, accepted, celebrated. To know what's driving us and why and to feel the freedom to say, *This is me! This is what I want. This is what I need. I know it and love that about myself!*

As I reached the peak of the trail and looked out over the vast Pacific, I felt a renewed sense of peace and purpose. To build the life of freedom I wanted, I had to embrace all of myself—the good, the so-called flawed, and everything in between. True freedom meant letting go of the pressure to be someone else and learning to fully own and celebrate who I was. I realized that this self-awareness wasn't just part of the journey; it was the foundation for making conscious, intentional choices about the life I wanted to create. I could see how knowing and celebrating myself would also likely lead to even more business and personal success as I wasted less time and energy trying to be someone I wasn't. As I started my descent, I felt a rush of energy and a bunch of ideas flooding in. *There I go,* I thought. *Seventeen new ideas before lunch—and I'll probably forget half of them by dinner.* But instead of criticizing myself, I just laughed, knowing, accepting, and loving that that's just part of who I am.

Know, Own, and Celebrate Yourself

As entrepreneurs, we often pride ourselves on being visionaries, trailblazers, and problem-solvers—the ones with the guts to try things others wouldn't even dream of. But beneath that, many of us struggle with something less glamorous: our relationship with ourselves. We are quick to criticize our actions, dismiss our emotions, and power through challenges without stopping to reflect. In the pursuit of success, we forget one critical piece of the puzzle: knowing and loving ourselves.

Self-awareness is the foundation of personal and professional growth, and it starts with curiosity and compassion—two qualities often missing in the high-pressure world of entrepreneurship. It's not that entrepreneurs lack curiosity; we're natural dreamers. But our curiosity often comes with a built-in critique. We judge ourselves harshly, expect perfection, and push forward with relentless drive—always measuring, always comparing.

But what if we traded that inner critic for a more open, compassionate curiosity? Instead of self-criticism, we could ask, *Interesting! What is this feeling telling me?* or *I wonder why I respond this way?*

And what if, instead of fighting our inner critic, we embraced it? *I love how critical I can be! I love my inner critic!* Shifting from criticism to curiosity and compassion gives us space to explore and understand ourselves deeply. The goal is not to judge or fix but to learn. By treating ourselves with compassion, we create freedom— the kind of freedom that allows us to see our behaviors as valuable data, not flaws.

Acceptance is a good start, but celebration is what gives us power. When you move from acceptance to celebration and true self-love, you begin to take pride in your unique qualities—not as flaws to fix or quirks to manage but as gifts to honor, amplify, and share.

This kind of celebration isn't about inflating your ego or becoming self-important. It's about recognizing your strengths, abilities, and achievements—even the small ones—and using them as fuel for growth. It's shifting your mindset from *I guess this is just who*

I am to *This is who I am. I love it and I'm proud of it.* This type of self-awareness allows you to fully step into your power and make better decisions to help you get more of what you want: more success, more meaning, more wealth, better relationships, more freedom.

How Do You Do This?

Celebrating yourself starts with **noticing**.

- Take time to **acknowledge wins**, no matter how small. Did you stay calm during a tough conversation? Did you follow through on something you wanted to avoid? Celebrate that.

- Practice **gratitude for yourself**. Write down what you appreciate about yourself—your courage, your creativity, your resilience —and review it often.

- Build a **highlight reel** of your successes. Reflect on the moments you're proud of, and remind yourself that those didn't happen by accident—you created them.

Start to see that your imperfections are not barriers to success but part of what makes you human, relatable, and real. When you honor what's good about yourself, you naturally let go of the constant need to prove yourself or to be everything to everyone.

The real shift happens when self-celebration becomes fuel—fuel to keep going, to stretch further, to take risks, and to trust that you have what it takes. You stop operating from scarcity and fear and instead start living from a place of abundance and confidence.

Science supports this. Eric Fields and Gina R. Kuperberg, researchers from the Department of Psychology at Tufts University, explain,

"Positively biased self-views are argued to be a key component of healthy psychological functioning, influencing self-esteem, motivation, and determination. Indeed, a lack of a self-positivity bias (or even a self-negativity bias) may contribute to mood and anxiety disorder."[7]

So celebrate yourself. Loudly. Quietly. In whatever way feels true to you. Because when you stop denying or just tolerating who you are and start honoring and celebrating yourself, that's when real freedom begins, and that may just lead to more success than you can imagine.

Values, Motivations, Preferences, and Tendencies

Once you begin to take a true interest in knowing yourself, start exploring the deeper motivations and values that guide your decisions and actions. As entrepreneurs, our values often align with creativity, innovation, and freedom. But beyond the obvious, what truly drives you?

- **Values:** What are the core principles that guide your decisions? For some, it's about leaving a lasting impact; for others, it might be about creating sustainable systems or prioritizing personal well-being or accomplishment. Understanding your values helps align your work with your deepest desires, making every action more meaningful.

- **Preferences and tendencies:** We all have different working styles and ways of approaching challenges. Do you thrive in chaos, or do you need structure? Do you prefer brainstorming alone or collaborating with a team? Recognizing your preferences can

---

7   Andleeb Asghar, "The Science of Self-Love: The Evidence-Based Benefits of Loving Yourself," Ness Labs, 2022, https://nesslabs.com/self-love.

help you design an environment that maximizes your productivity and joy.

Exploring these elements of yourself isn't just a feel-good exercise; it helps you show up more authentically in your work. When you know what you value and what motivates you, you can make decisions with clarity and confidence. You're less likely to chase inappropriate goals or feel pressured to meet someone else's expectations. Be aware of the judgments you may make, as in *These values are better or worse than others*. What if they just are what they are? Can you see them with curiosity, accept them with compassion, celebrate them with excitement, and work with them, not against them?

Challenges

While it's empowering to understand your strengths and motivations, it's equally important to acknowledge your challenges, your personal roadblocks. We all have limiting beliefs, blind spots, and unrealistic expectations that can hold us back.

- **Limiting beliefs:** These are the unconscious stories we tell ourselves that dictate what we believe is possible. Maybe you've convinced yourself you're not smart enough, experienced enough, or worthy of success. These beliefs are often remnants of past experiences and fears. To move past them, you must first recognize and refute them.

- **Blind spots:** We all have areas where we lack awareness. It might be our tendency to overlook details or avoid conflict. Blind spots can derail us if we're not aware of them. Seeking feedback from others can help reveal these blind spots so you can address them head-on. Our biggest problems in life are not what we confront but what we avoid.

- **Personal expectations:** Entrepreneurs tend to set extremely high expectations for themselves. This is both a blessing and a curse. While it can drive you to succeed, it can also lead to burn-out and a perpetual feeling of inadequacy. Learning to manage these expectations is critical for long-term sustainability.

By acknowledging your challenges, you take the first step in overcoming them. You're no longer avoiding or denying them but seeing them as part of your reality. This self-awareness leads to better decisions and more authentic actions that are more likely to lead to success the way you choose to define it.

When Strengths Become Weaknesses

One of the most insidious traps entrepreneurs fall into is letting their strengths transform into weaknesses. A classic example is optimism. While optimism is a powerful trait that keeps entrepreneurs moving forward in the face of uncertainty, unchecked optimism can be a major blind spot. If you're overly optimistic, you may ignore red flags or fail to prepare for potential risks. This is where self-derailment comes into play.

The psychology pioneer Carl Jung famously said that the "shadow" is the part of ourselves we refuse to acknowledge. It's the part of us that we project onto the world, blaming external forces for our internal fears. To achieve true wholeness, we must own our shadows. In the case of strengths becoming weaknesses, it means recognizing when our strengths—like ambition, confidence, or perseverance—are driving us toward unhealthy patterns.

Take confidence, for example: It can easily turn into arrogance, leading us to overestimate our abilities or ignore advice from others. Perseverance can morph into stubbornness, making it hard to pivot when necessary.

I experienced this firsthand after my success with ZICO. Building and selling the company gave me an overly optimistic view of my ability to make smart investments. I thought I had the Midas touch—until a few investments turned to lead. It didn't take long to realize that evaluating businesses required a completely different skill set, which I had to work to develop.

By owning these tendencies—both strengths and weaknesses—we gain the awareness to recognize when they're helping us stay on course or quietly pulling us off track. And with that awareness, we can adjust and course correct before it's too late.

Seeking and Receiving Feedback

Entrepreneurship can be lonely, especially when people hesitate to offer honest feedback. That's why becoming a feedback junkie is essential. Seeking input regularly—from your team, mentors, and peers—helps reveal blind spots, refine your approach, and improve how you show up.

When asking for feedback, set the stage: Express your openness while acknowledging your tendency to get defensive. A simple way to ensure you're listening is to repeat back what you've heard: "What I hear you saying is _____. Did I get that right?" If you feel defensive, great; you've found something to learn from.

I ask for feedback constantly, even from junior team members. To encourage honesty, I make it specific: "How could I be more supportive and effective for you?" The more you ask, the more people share—and that's when real growth happens.

Of course, feedback can sting. If you feel yourself reacting, try this: "I appreciate this, but I feel defensive. Can we pick this up later?" This keeps the conversation open without forcing immediate processing.

The goal isn't to change with every critique but to gather data, see yourself through another's eyes, and reflect on what resonates. At a minimum, it shows how you're perceived, which may surprise you.

Feedback is just information—it's neither good nor bad. What matters is how you process it. Does it ring true? If so, how can you use it to grow?

Pairing external feedback with self-reflection—through journaling, meditation, or personality tools—creates a powerful loop for growth. The more you seek feedback, the more self-aware you become, driving continuous learning, better leadership, and greater freedom.

FREEDOM TOOL:
Seven Peak Moments of Freedom

In this exercise, you'll look back over your life and identify seven specific milestones or experiences where you felt truly free and alive. These could be from your work, personal life, hobbies, projects, or relationships. Here's how to capture those standout moments:

- **Pick seven peak moments:** When did you feel a deep sense of freedom? Write down a sentence or two to capture the moment.

- **Why is this significant to you?** What was meaningful to you personally?

- **What were your specific achievements?** What made each moment special?

- **What was great about it?** What was enjoyable, fulfilling, or satisfying about this? How did that sense of freedom feel to you?

- **How did you create this?** How did you get involved, create, or cocreate it?

- **What were the key steps?** Outline the steps you took to bring this moment to life.

COMMON THREADS

With the above, take a step back and look for common threads, such as

- ▸ A thirst for adventure
- ▸ A knack for leadership
- ▸ A talent for troubleshooting or stepping into tough situations

- An ability to inspire and motivate others
- Joy in seeing others grow through your mentorship
- A penchant for creativity

IDENTIFY YOUR STRONGEST COMPETENCIES

From these threads, what are the strongest competencies you demonstrated? What skills and talents are your greatest? Examples might include

- Leading and inspiring others
- Team building
- Intuitive decision-making
- Resolving conflicts
- Taking an idea from concept to launch

Consider sharing this with others and asking for their feedback on the themes they hear. Their insights might help you gain a clearer understanding of your unique strengths and gifts.

This exercise is more than just celebrating your past achievements; it's about knowing your strengths and understanding how you can leverage them in your journey forward. Embrace your moments of freedom, and let them guide you toward a future filled with even more success and liberating experiences. Hold on to this: You may want it as part of your Freedom Binder (we'll talk more about that later) so you can remind yourself what you accomplished and check in with yourself when considering new opportunities.

THE TAKEAWAYS
Step 2: Know, Own, and Celebrate Yourself

What's the Point?

Knowing yourself, owning your needs and challenges, and celebrating your strengths unlock clarity, courage, and the power to freely pursue whatever it is you desire.

Why Is This Important?

Freedom requires self-awareness and self-love. When you stop criticizing yourself (or at least love the critic in you) and start getting curious, compassionate, and intentional, you gain the power to own your values, strengths, and challenges—turning insecurities into assets.

How To: Start Knowing, Owning, and Celebrating Yourself

- **Track patterns and reactions:** Notice what energizes or drains you. Ask, *What's working? What's not?* Awareness is the first step to growth.

- **Identify peak moments:** Reflect on times you've felt proud, alive, or fulfilled. These highlight your core values and strengths.

- **Celebrate small wins:** Build confidence by seeing progress, not just perfection.

Go Deeper

- **Books:**
  - ▸ *Learning to Love Yourself* by Gay Hendricks
  - ▸ *The Gifts of Imperfection* by Brené Brown

- **Tools (markrampolla.co):**
  - ▸ Values Clarification Exercise
  - ▸ Zone of Genius
  - ▸ Personality Tests (Myers-Briggs, Enneagram, Hogan, DISC)
  - ▸ 360-Degree Feedback

What's Next?

With a clearer sense of who you are, it's time to break free from limiting beliefs and patterns. Step 3 is about releasing what's holding you back so you can step fully into freedom.

BREAK FREE OF WHAT HOLDS YOU BACK

Soon after selling ZICO, my mother's health began to fail. I asked my parents if they wanted to move from Pittsburgh to California to be closer to us. They agreed, and we bought them a condo a mile from our house, just across the street from the beach. It was a bit lavish for my dad's taste—he said he'd be just fine in a broom closet but knew my mother would appreciate being near the ocean. Being close to two of his granddaughters, whom he absolutely adored, certainly helped, as did the chance to escape Pittsburgh winters.

One evening, we all sat around our new home's outdoor sunken firepit, watching the sunset over the Pacific. Maura and I invited my parents to a party the following weekend to meet some of our friends.

"This will be good for you, Don," my mom said, nudging my dad. "You can finally get over your last prejudice."

He looked at her, confused. "Prejudice? Toward whom?"

"Rich people," she replied with a smile.

My dad shrugged. "I just haven't met any who are good people."

My dad was by no means alone in that respect. Studies taken in several countries have found that rich individuals "are predominantly portrayed as cold-hearted, profit-hungry, and morally suspect."[8]

My dad had a complex relationship with money, which I didn't fully appreciate for a long time. He had grown up modestly, and though he was highly educated—a PhD in nuclear physics—he chose a life rooted in values over wealth.

The wealthy, in his mind, were selfish and out of touch with the real struggles of life. In truth, he probably hadn't met many rich people in Pittsburgh, but he certainly lived by his own definition of "good."

When I was growing up, he would often bring strangers home for dinner—people whose cars had broken down or who were homeless. Neighbors knew the Rampollas were an odd bunch—no white bread, sugar cereals, or Skippy in our house, and every time there was a major snowstorm, my Dad, brothers, and I would patrol the neighborhood like a volunteer rescue squad, shovels in hand, ready to dig cars out of snowbanks.

Dad brought kids from a Black family along with us to our still-segregated community pool. My parents invited an unwed teenage mother to live with us for months when she had nowhere else to go.

Dinner table conversations? Oh, we kept it light—topics like the murder of Jesuits in El Salvador, economic injustice, and CEO greed. You know, classic mealtime banter. Dad never missed a chance to teach a lesson.

Intellectually, my dad was brilliant. He made a good living, but he never rose to the executive ranks, likely making little more than the steelworkers who lived nearby. He had his principles, and he stuck by them.

Yet for a man who could split atoms, he struggled to manage his

---

8   Rainer Zitelmann, "Upward Classism: Prejudice and Stereotyping Against the Wealthy," *Economic Affairs* 40 (2020): 162–79, https://doi.org/10.1111/ecaf.12407.

own finances. He despised the stock market—probably because it refused to follow the laws of physics. Even worse, he was an experimental investor, testing theories like *What happens if you buy at the peak and sell at the bottom?* The results were exactly what you'd expect. He passed away nearly broke, leaving behind a financial mess for us to untangle. My dad wasn't just bad with money; he treated it like radioactive material, something best handled from a safe distance or not at all. Inherently dangerous.

Mom was right. As kind, gentle, and generous as my father was, he had a deep-seated prejudice against those with money. This attitude, combined with his financial disorganization, shaped much of his life—and, as I later realized, also influenced mine.

For years, I hadn't thought about the impact his views on wealth had on me. But as I reflected, I began to see the connections. I could see from a young age I felt guilty about my drive and ambition. "The meek shall inherit the earth," according to the Bible and, "It's harder for a rich man to get into Heaven than a camel through the eye of the needle." So basically, if I wanted to be successful and wealthy, I was doomed to lose both Heaven and earth.

I had pursued a business career, yet I chose to go to a Jesuit university—one of the religious orders my dad admired. I joined the Peace Corps after college, and later, I got a dual degree in business and environmental management, because an MBA alone would scream greed, but add "environmental management" and suddenly it's social justice in a suit. I chose to live and work in El Salvador, the country my parents spoke about years earlier. Coincidence? Or was I unknowingly turning my life into an extended tribute to my dad's values—minus the snow shoveling?

During a session with my therapist, I opened up about how much I valued the financial security that came from selling ZICO—and the freedom it gave me. I also admitted my relentless drive to do more, build more, and make more money. Then I paused and said, "At the same time, I wonder—do I already have too much? Have I always wanted too much? How much is enough? Sometimes I think I should just give it all away and devote myself to peace and justice."

Agnes listened, then said, "Before you make any big decisions, let's unpack what's really driving this. If, after that, you still want to give it all away, great. But first, let me ask: Are you sure this is what you want? Or is this your father's fantasy?"

That question hit hard. Was I really ready to trade financial freedom for a vow of poverty—or was I just playing out some monk fantasy I thought my dad might respect? You know: barefoot, robes, tending a garden, and debating theology over lentil soup and mead. I realized that, unconsciously, I had inherited his belief system about money, success, and power, even though I hadn't consciously embraced it. But knowing it was one thing; breaking free from it was another.

I began to ask: Could I allow myself to embrace wealth without guilt? Did I have an upper limit on how much wealth was OK? Could I enjoy success without feeling it was inherently corrupt? Could I, in fact, be wealthy and still be kind, loving, and generous? Could I be monk-like—but in the business world and with a nice house, fun cars, great food, and summers in Europe?

I began to see these were limiting beliefs—handed down from my father—that were holding me back. Over time, I began to flip those beliefs on their head. Instead of thinking of money and power as a burden or a source of guilt, I started seeing it as a tool for doing more good in the world. What if wealth gave me the freedom to create even more impact? And what was wrong with just appreciating and celebrating the richness of life with friends and family, or even by myself?

The key realization? Wealth wasn't the problem. The problem was the irrational belief that money and goodness couldn't coexist—and that enjoying money automatically made you a sellout. Once I saw that, I understood something freeing: I could pursue what I wanted, make as much money as I allowed myself to make—or not—and still be true to myself.

I don't blame my dad. He lived by his values and did his best to live his life on his terms. But I'm my own person. I'm not destined to take a vow of poverty or live off lentil soup in a monastery. I can strive for and love success, build wealth, and still make an impact and be true to myself.

If all this was true, what else was holding me back? What other limiting beliefs did I need to let go of to live my life to the fullest? Plenty. I could see I still had a lot of work to do—but at least now I had a playbook that didn't require a vow of poverty.

Resistance to Freedom: Letting Go to Break Free

Letting go has never come naturally to me—and let's be honest, it's not something most entrepreneurs embrace. We're not exactly known for "letting it be." As a rule, we push, hustle, and obsess over outcomes. We fight like hell to stay in control—of our businesses, our teams, and, let's face it, our identities.

Our ego resists letting go through skepticism, distraction, or justification. We vent, rationalize, and double down on why we need to hold on to negative emotions, fears, or outdated beliefs. But as David Hawkins explains in his fantastic book *Letting Go*, resistance is actually progress.[9] When we challenge the ego's grip, it pushes back—and that's the beginning part of the process of letting go.

Hawkins points out that resistance is often driven by fear of losing

---

9   David Hawkins, *Letting Go: The Pathway of Surrender* (Hay House, 2014): 34.

control or identity.[10] For entrepreneurs, this hits especially hard. Our identities are often tied directly to our businesses. That was certainly true for me during my time building ZICO.

For most of ZICO's journey, I did everything I could to control the outcome—every day, every week, every month, every year. That's what I thought it took to win. My identity was so closely tied to ZICO that I became "the ZICO guy." In many ways, the brand and I were one and the same.

I had a deep fear of losing control of the business—and resisted even admitting there were aspects of it I couldn't control. It was as if I equated letting go with failure or irrelevance. I see it all the time—founders so tied to their role and identity as "founder and CEO" that they can't surrender any of it. I'm not suggesting you give it all up—but you can't control everything. And the harder you try, the tighter those chains become.

The Power of Letting Go

Hawkins says—and I've experienced it firsthand—that when we examine and let go of these fears, the resistance itself dissolves.[11] Letting go isn't foreign or unnatural. It's instinctive.

Think of a dog doing a full-body shake after barking like crazy. It doesn't overthink it; it just shakes off the tension and moves on. When we stop overthinking and allow ourselves to let go, we create space for freedom, clarity, and growth.

I saw this play out during a particularly challenging situation at one of our portfolio companies. I had taken on a sort of lead role on the board of directors—I was the oldest and most experienced and

---

10 Hawkins, *Letting Go*, 74.
11 Hawkins, *Letting Go*, 169, 187.

naturally assumed that meant I should take lead. I felt like it was my role to have all the answers.

But I did something different. Instead of driving the conversation or insisting I knew best, I resisted the urge to try to control the process. I let other board members and others on my team take the lead. I focused on containing my thoughts and creating space to see what happened. I surrendered.

What happened? The group delivered better results than I ever could have imagined. Not only did I feel greater energy and clarity, but I also saw the power of trust and surrender. And others seized the opportunity to step up, learn, and grow in their own style of leadership and sense of power.

Letting go didn't mean checking out. I remained highly engaged and present. It meant stepping back just enough to allow others to step up. And when they did, we saw the ripple effects: better decisions, a stronger group dynamic, and better results in the business.

Over time, in situation after situation, I began to see that often, the more I could let go of my desire to control, the better the results. There is a time and place to step up and lead, and there is a time and place to step back, observe, and surrender.

Test it out and see. You might be blown away by what happens.

Sounds great, but how? you may ask. I'll show you what worked for me in the Freedom Key tool at the end of this chapter.

Letting Go Of . . .

Letting go in key areas can be especially powerful—though not always easy for entrepreneurs. But by releasing what holds us back, we create space for growth, freedom, and even greater results than we ever imagined.

The Past

The past can be a trap—whether through painful memories, nostalgia for "the good times," or outdated visions of success. Even what once inspired us can become a limitation if we refuse to evolve.

Letting go isn't about forgetting; it's about recognizing that clinging—even to positive moments—can hold us back. What once served us may no longer fit who we are or where we're going. It's like driving forward while staring in the rearview mirror: The scenery might be familiar, but eventually, you'll crash.

For years, I applied lessons from ZICO to every new business I was involved with. That approach worked—until it didn't. I had to let go of seeing ZICO as my ultimate success story—the all-applicable prototype—to make room for something even bigger. Clinging to its success risked limiting my future.

True freedom comes when we stop living in past stories—good or bad—and start embracing what's possible now.

Limiting Beliefs

Limiting beliefs are the unconscious stories we tell ourselves—things like *I'm not smart enough, I don't have the right skills,* or *I can't succeed.* And if we do succeed? We write it off as luck.

Competing beliefs make it even harder. *I want to be successful, but success means I won't be happy.* These internal conflicts keep us stuck in fear and second-guessing.

I held the belief that *I'm not really a great CEO* when I compared my success at ZICO with that of other entrepreneurs who had built even bigger beverage businesses. I turned it around into *I'm so glad I gained experience running businesses and now get to learn from others who did it differently, both of which make me a better investor and advisor.*

Letting go of limiting beliefs isn't just about releasing doubts;

it's about replacing them with empowering narratives. This process opens the door to bigger opportunities.

Anger, Blame, Fear, and Pride

So-called negative emotions like anger, fear, and pride carry tremendous energy. Properly channeled, they can create change. Left unchecked, they keep us stuck in reactivity.

Anger can turn into blame—pointing fingers instead of taking responsibility. But when we stop resisting anger and feel it fully, it naturally dissipates. It may come back, but it can always be released again.

Fear, often more subtle, holds us back from risks, goals, and growth. Sometimes, fear is a gift that keeps us safe, but other times, it paralyzes us. Awareness helps us discern which it is and choose the best path forward.

Pride is another hidden trap. It can inflate our ego, making us defensive and resistant to feedback. Letting go of pride means embracing humility and vulnerability, which lead to deeper growth and connection.

Relationships

Not all relationships are meant to last forever. Some can stifle growth and keep us tethered to the past. Letting go of relationships—whether personal or professional—doesn't have to be bitter. It's about releasing emotional ties and setting healthy boundaries.

I saw this at ZICO. Early service providers were critical to our success, but as we scaled, some weren't the right fit. We had to make tough calls. Some relationships evolved with us; others didn't—and parting ways with those that no longer served us was necessary to be even more successful.

I've seen many entrepreneurs held back by their relationships with early team members, partners, or vendors who no longer fit their current and future needs and vision. Growth requires making space for relationships that support where you're headed, not where you've been. Sometimes it's necessary to end relationships that no longer serve you, even if you haven't found the new ones yet. Saying no to good relationships to leave room for great ones isn't a value judgment about the people themselves, just the needs of you and your business.

Expectations and Perfectionism

Entrepreneurs often set high expectations—for themselves and others. But rigid attachment to specific outcomes can lead to frustration, disappointment, and guilt when things don't go as planned.

We're imperfect. What we do is imperfect. Entrepreneurs weigh trade-offs, make choices, and deal with the consequences. You won't make everyone happy.

What if your imperfections create opportunities for others to step into their strengths? What if your expectations are actually holding your team back from creativity and breakthrough ideas?

What if the future could be even bigger and better than we envisioned? By letting go of perfectionism and embracing progress, we give ourselves the freedom to create something beyond what we may have imagined possible.

Letting Go of Fundamental Human Desires: Acknowledgment, Control, and Security

In *The Sedona Method*, Hale Dwoskin highlights how our desires for acknowledgment, control, and security often keep us emotionally chained.[12] We crave recognition, seek control over circumstances, and chase security through external means—but these desires often lead to stress, anxiety, and dependence.

Acknowledgment is one of the strongest desires. We look to others for validation, but relying on external praise gives others power over our emotions. Dwoskin teaches us to become our own source of acknowledgment, building inner self-worth that isn't tied to outside approval.

Control is another trap. Life is unpredictable, and clinging to control only creates tension. Letting go opens us to trust the process and adapt more easily.

Similarly, the pursuit of security can leave us stuck in fear and scarcity. True security doesn't come from guarantees; it comes from trusting ourselves to handle uncertainty as it arises.

Recognizing these patterns has been incredibly powerful for me. But even after recognizing them, I still struggled with what to do with that awareness. I began to wonder, *How can I take that awareness, make sense of it, and act upon it to bring myself back to a place of freedom?* After using various techniques, including the Sedona Method, The Work by Byron Katie, and practices from Gay Hendricks and The Conscious Leadership Group, I developed my own "tool" that I have found allows me to deal with even the most intense emotional experience and shift back to a state of freedom. I call it the Freedom Key.

---

12 Hale Dwoskin, *The Sedona Method: Your Key to Lasting Happiness, Success, Peace, and Emotional Well-Being* (Sedona Press, 2003).

FREEDOM TOOL: The Freedom Key

The Freedom Key

! **Triggered?**
React
Escape
Defend

Breathe

Repeat as needed

1 What are you **Thinking?**
Is it True?

2 What are you **Feeling?**
Name and Locate

3 What do you **Want?**
Acknowledgement, Control, Security

4 Can you **Let Go?**
If now now, when?

Back to Freedom
Aware   Open
Curious Present

If you feel reactive, defensive, or in other ways triggered or trapped by an experience or situation, use the Freedom Key to shift back to freedom. Pick a trigger in your life, big or small, that carries strong feelings. Target someone specific, if possible (not you, to start).

Take a slow, steady breath. Consider the situation. As an example, let's go back to the situation in which Dan and I were debating whether to make an investment. I felt strongly that we should go for it. Dan didn't agree. I left the conversation feeling frustrated, misunderstood, and stuck. This is how I might use the Freedom Key to shift back to a state of freedom.

Step 1: What am I thinking?

I take a breath and sit with the situation. Then, I write down my thoughts:

- *Dan should trust my instincts. I've done this before!*
- *He shouldn't be so cautious; he's playing it too safe.*
- *I can't believe I'm having to defend myself! I must be terrible at explaining things.*

- *If this investment doesn't happen, it's going to be a missed opportunity, and if we miss out on this, we might not achieve the results we want in this fund or the firm.*

Are these stories true? Am I certain?

I pause. *No, not really.* I'm not certain Dan doesn't trust me; maybe he just needed more information. And maybe his caution isn't fear; it's thoughtful skepticism.

Play it all the way out

I let my mind go as far and dramatic as it wants to. *What if Dan never agrees? What if we lose this opportunity, the company tanks, and I'm labeled the guy who blew it? What if I end up broke, living in my car?*

OK. That made me laugh—and I could already feel some tension releasing.

Step 2: What am I feeling? Where do I feel it in my body?

I ask myself, *What am I really feeling?*

- *Frustration.* I notice tightness in my chest.

- *Anger.* I experience that as heat in my face and neck.

- *Fear.* Fear of being wrong or being seen as incompetent.

I notice how naming the emotions helps me start to separate myself from them. They aren't me; they are just energy moving through my body, like clouds passing in the sky.

Step 3: What do I want? Acknowledgment? Control? Security?

I can see all three desires, but really, I want **acknowledgment**—to feel like my thoughts and experience are respected by someone I respect, Dan.

Step 4: Can I let go?

I ask myself, *Can I let this go? If not now, when?*

I can challenge the story

- *What if Dan's pushback is happening* for *me? What if it forces me to strengthen my argument, fill in the gaps, and make sure this investment is really the right move?*

I can turn it around

- *What if Dan isn't doubting me? What if he is actually protecting us both from jumping in too fast? Can I see I'm really doubting myself? Can I love my inner critic?*

I can give myself what I want

- *I take a breath and remind myself, I can be my own source of acknowledgement. I am experienced. I've made good calls before. I can trust myself, even if Dan doesn't see it yet.*

I can release the tension physically

- *I stand up, stretch, and shake out my arms—letting go of this whole story like a dog shaking off water. It might feel weird, but it usually works. My body relaxes, and so does my mind.*

To make this practice second nature, I use a simple memory technique: *I think and feel I want to be free.* It helps me remember the key steps in the moment: Pause to recognize my thoughts, notice my emotions, identify what I'm seeking, and then let go. The more I use it, the faster I shift back to freedom.

THE TAKEAWAYS
Step 3: Breaking Free of What Holds You Back

What's the Point?

The beliefs, stories, and patterns we carry often create invisible prisons, keeping us stuck. When we break free from these mental traps, we create space for peace, joy, and the ability to create more of what we want, including even greater success on our own terms.

Why Is This Important?

Releasing what no longer serves us helps us reclaim our power to choose how we respond in each situation, regardless of what we think and feel—unlocking deeper confidence, clarity, and possibility.

How To: Break Free of What Holds You Back

- **Notice and challenge your stories:** Use the Freedom Key to question your thoughts.

- **Process your emotions:** Don't bury emotions; explore them. Notice what you're feeling and where it shows up in your body. Naming emotions reduces their power.

- **Let go and shift your focus:** Ask, *What if the opposite is true? If I can't let go now, when can I?*

Go Deeper

- **Books:**
  - ▸ *The Untethered Soul* by Michael A. Singer
  - ▸ *Letting Go* by David R. Hawkins

- **Tools (markrampolla.co):**
  - ▸ Limiting Belief Release Practice
  - ▸ Say No to Good to Leave Room for Great
  - ▸ Clean Up Excercise

What's Next?

Now that you've learned how to let go of limiting beliefs, it's time to take bold, intentional action. In Step 4, we'll explore how to dream bigger, take risks, and step confidently into the life you're ready to create.

FREE TO DREAM

We met in front of my old house, Marcus stepping out of his black Porsche Cayenne, dressed in his signature style: a big black brimmed hat, black T-shirt, black pants, black tennis shoes with white soles, and black sunglasses. He looked every bit the musician he was. But when he took off his sunglasses, the austere look softened—his kind eyes and welcoming smile broke through.

I had met Marcus less than a year prior, and we had quickly become close friends. A child entrepreneur and musical prodigy, he had gone on to produce for top artists before venturing into crypto and AI, where he had done exceptionally well. Now, he and his new partner were considering buying a house in one of the beach communities of the South Bay, and he had asked me to show him around.

As I opened the gate—built from a wooden mandala we had brought back from Bali—the lush front yard welcomed us. It looked exactly as I had once envisioned: beautiful clay pots overflowing with bougainvillea and succulents, a rustic shade structure I had designed. Funny, though—I had always imagined living here to enjoy it, not just visiting like a guest on a home tour.

We stepped up to the house, and I pushed open the massive wooden door. The narrow hallway spilled into a breathtaking view of the sky and ocean, a sight that still felt like stepping into another world.

Marcus took it in, eyes wide. "Wow, this is incredible," he said.

Maura, my soon-to-be-ex-wife, came down the stairs with her usual bubbly energy, greeting me and then Marcus with big hugs. We had separated a few months before and, overall, were navigating it well—untangling our marriage while redefining our relationship and family.

As they chatted, I wandered through the house, feeling a mix of nostalgia and sadness. This place had been an inspirational refuge, filled with both beautiful memories and the quiet ache of our separation. It was strange—like visiting an old friend's house, only to realize you once owned all the furniture.

Marcus gravitated toward the grand piano in the living room, effortlessly blending jazz and funk as he played. I knelt down to give Titus a long-overdue belly rub before leading Marcus on a tour, from the upper deck to the sunken firepit overlooking the ocean.

We made our way down to the lower yard in front of the Rancho. The once-grass-filled yard was now a sprawling succulent garden, accented with driftwood and rocks I had hauled up from the beach hundreds of feet below—my version of a Spartan race.

We settled into the Adirondack chairs I had designed and built with one of the carpenters who worked on our house, gazing out at the ocean stretching endlessly before us. I told Marcus I had decided to let Maura keep the house. As much as I loved it, living by the beach had always been her dream. But she realized maintaining it alone was too much, so we had agreed to sell. I turned to Marcus and said, "I'm gonna miss this place."

Marcus paused, taking in the vast Pacific. Then, with a smirk, he said, "Not bad . . . for a warm-up act."

I glanced at him, wanting to punch him and hug him. Part of me thought, *Are you kidding? I worked my whole life to get here!* Coming from Pittsburgh to a beachfront home in California—what more could I want? But another part of me knew the truth: I was stuck. Maura and I had both thought this was our forever home, to match our forever marriage. Neither was true anymore, and I had no idea what I wanted next.

"What do you mean?" I asked.

Marcus just smiled. "Maybe it's time to start dreaming again, Mark. You did this once. If you want to do it again, you can. Do you want something bigger? Something different? Whatever you want, you know how to create it. It starts with a dream."

I stood up, and so did he. I wrapped him in a bear hug and said, "Thank you, my friend. I think that's exactly what I needed to hear."

The Power of a Dream

That conversation with Marcus sparked deep reflection. As we sat overlooking the Pacific, I realized I had achieved nearly everything I once set out to do in starting ZICO. What began as a far-fetched dream had become reality. I had built ZICO into a multimillion-dollar company, created a new beverage category, and sold the business to Coca-Cola—securing financial rewards for myself, my family, and my investors beyond what I had originally imagined.

Maura and I had also shared a strong marriage for many years and raised two wonderful daughters. I had so much to be proud of—so much that was once only a dream. And yet, sitting there with Marcus, I realized something unsettling—I had stopped dreaming.

The dreams I had back in 2004, including having a beautiful home on the beach, were powerful motivators. I always held those in mind and tracked my progress relentlessly, breaking goals into daily, weekly, and monthly actions. That focus and persistence kept me moving forward, even in the toughest times. And it worked.

Not everything had gone as planned. ZICO wasn't yet the global brand I had envisioned, and my marriage hadn't lasted. Yet, looking back, what I had accomplished was extraordinary—far beyond what I imagined growing up in Pittsburgh or what most of my family and friends expected of me.

And then I hit a wall. With so many of my dreams realized, I had started to coast. Without a clear vision of what was next, I felt unmoored. It turns out we all need dreams; they're what drive us. Without one, I felt restless and aimless.

But sitting there with Marcus, I could feel that drive stirring again. I wasn't done. There was more to accomplish in business, more to learn about myself, and more impact I wanted to make in health, wellness, and sustainability. I wanted to build more wealth, both for what it could empower me to do and—I could now own—just because I wanted it.

It wasn't about buying a bigger house, although I'd need one eventually. It was about what a house represented: a new chapter, freedom, success, and a fresh start. That applied to my career, my personal growth, and maybe even finding love again someday.

Marcus was right. It was time to dream again. Dreams are powerful: They drive us to take risks, build businesses, and create meaningful lives. Without them, we drift. But when we embrace them, we unlock the potential to build something greater than we ever imagined.

Dreams don't have to be a one-time deal. It was time to tap into that power again—and this time, dream even bigger.

From Dream to Reality

Dreams, goals, desires, objectives, intentions—whatever you call them, they've been part of the human experience since the dawn of time. Explorers sought uncharted lands, individuals strove for wealth or spiritual growth, and countless people have pursued their own visions of success and freedom. Yet why do so many struggle to achieve their dreams? This question is especially relevant for entrepreneurs, with the 90 percent failure rate of start-ups.

Entrepreneurial dreams aren't limited to building successful businesses. We dream about financial stability, health, adventure, and shared goals with partners, family, and friends. Yet many people stumble in three key areas: the goal-setting process, the goals themselves, and execution. Additionally, most fail to leverage their whole being—mind, body, and soul. Let's start with that.

Leveraging Your Entire Being to Achieve Your Dreams

Entrepreneurs often approach goals intellectually, relying heavily on their brain power. But why not engage your entire self? Regardless of your natural tendencies—whether you are head focused, intuitive, or heart centered—you can benefit from tools like visualization and even what I call *emotionalization*.

Visualization and emotionalization allow you to create a full-body experience of what freedom looks and feels like. By vividly imagining yourself living the life you desire, you bring that sensory experience into the present. This process influences your mindset, helping you align your actions with your dreams. We'll dive deeper into this exercise later, but for now, remember: Freedom isn't just something you think about; it's something you feel, embody, and actively pursue.

The Goal-Setting Process

Setting goals can be fraught with emotions, past experiences, and misconceptions. Many entrepreneurs start with grand visions of success and freedom but quickly become bogged down by reality. Why? Often, it's because of emotional baggage.

For some, past failures create doubt, leading to beliefs like *This never works* or *I'm no good at this*. Others start with disbelief, feeling their dream is too far-fetched or unrealistic. On the flip side, prior success can create overconfidence, blinding us to the challenges ahead.

To set yourself up for success, approach goal setting with as much clarity and freedom from the past as possible. Let go of preconceived notions about what's "realistic" or whether you're "good" or "bad" at achieving goals. Start fresh, with an open mind.

Problems with the Goals Themselves

The content of your goals can also be limiting. Many people get trapped by societal "shoulds" and "shouldn'ts." For example, you might believe that career or financial goals are worthy while personal aspirations are frivolous. Can you allow yourself to pursue what truly matters to you, without judgment?

Sometimes, the emotions tied to a dream make it feel too overwhelming to pursue. Other times, you might dismiss your goal as too big or too small to be worth the effort. Recognize that wanting multiple things doesn't mean you need to chase them all at once— or even at all. Discernment is a powerful precursor to execution. Prioritize what truly matters, and focus your energy there.

Additonally, your goals change over time, whereas your values— which many of us rarely define or use as guides for our goals—may be more enduring.

The Execution Problem

The biggest obstacle to entrepreneurs achieving their goals is usually execution. Ideas are easy; execution is tough. We romanticize simplistic slogans like "Just do it," but the reality is far more complex. Execution requires time, effort, persistence, and often pivoting and changing direction.

We frequently overestimate what we can achieve in a year and underestimate what we can accomplish in ten. Success comes from sustained effort, not quick wins. Before diving into execution, consider whether you carry beliefs about being "good" or "bad" at following through. Let those go, and approach the process with curiosity and a willingness to learn.

Another key barrier is attachment to outcomes. Many people see goals as all-or-nothing propositions: Either they succeed, or they fail entirely. This mindset creates unnecessary pressure. Letting go of rigid expectations often leads to better results. And remember: Even if you don't achieve a certain goal, chances are good you're closer to it than before. Similarly, pursuing goals to avoid unwanted outcomes—like financial struggles—can backfire. Focusing on what you don't want tends to bring more of it into your life.

Execution also requires flexibility. Even when you don't achieve exactly what you set out to do, the process itself can lead to unexpected opportunities. Sometimes, what emerges is better than what you originally imagined. The key is to stay open, allowing your goals to evolve naturally.

Turning Dreams into Reality

Achieving your dreams isn't just about setting and hitting targets; it's about remaining adaptable and present throughout the journey. Goals are valuable tools, but they're not fixed destinations. Whether you achieve, exceed, or fall short of your objectives, what matters most is how you engage with the process.

By leveraging your entire being, freeing yourself from past limitations, and staying flexible in execution, you can turn your dreams into reality—often in ways you never expected. Freedom isn't a distant ideal; it's woven into every step you take toward your goals. Let it guide you, and watch as your dreams unfold.

FREEDOM TOOL: From Dream to Reality

Step 1: Visualize and Emotionalize Your Freedom

Take thirty to sixty minutes for this exercise in a quiet, distraction-free space. Visualize your best life—the one in which you are truly free.

Picture waking up completely rested in a serene space that reflects your style and values. Maybe the sunlight filters through your window as you stretch, feeling energized and at peace. Mentally, you are sharp and free from unnecessary worries, ready to embrace a day aligned with your values and choices. Where are you? Maybe it's not exact, but is it urban? Rural? Mountainous? Hot? Cold? Are you alone, or with someone? There is no right or wrong. This is your vision!

What is your morning routine? Coffee? A workout? Mediation? A walk in nature? There is no right. No wrong. This is your dream, no one else's.

What is your ideal work routine? Are you in an office? Working from home? Alone or with others? Is it consistent or varied? What sort of hours do you work?

Imagine you feel connected and engaged. You have a sense of purpose. Throughout the day, your energy flows effortlessly, and each moment feels intentional and fulfilling. What are you doing? What are you working toward? Who are you doing it with? What is your role versus others'? Again, there is no right or wrong. What do you see? What do you feel?

Financially, you feel secure and abundant, with the resources to live comfortably and pursue your passions. You feel healthy and have ample energy. How have you made that happen?

Throughout your day, you savor moments of pure joy. What are you doing? Enjoying a meal, reading a good book, or marveling at nature?

How do you end your day? Again, there is no right or wrong.

Are you alone? With others? Watching a movie? Reading a book? Making dinner? Ordering in? Eating out?

Life feels balanced, flowing naturally as you relish both the journey and the destination. How do you end your night?

Put yourself there. Don't imagine. Be there. Time travel. Maybe you feel it, sense it, see it? However you can express it is perfect. Stay there as long as you like, and revisit often.

Step 2: Craft Freedom Goals

- **Define freedom and success on your terms:** Define what success and freedom mean to *you*. They may change over time, but let them reflect *your* dreams, *your* values, not the expectations of others.

- **Phrase your goals in the present tense, and make them positive:** Phrase them as though you are already living them, and state what you want rather than what you're trying to avoid.

- **Make your goals right for you:** Start small, and make your goals achievable. Freedom is a momentum game: Put up a few wins, and then you can dream bigger.

- **Consider freedom in all areas of life:** Consider your health, relationships, community, and personal growth so that you create a holistic, financial, and professional sense of freedom.

- **Be specific while allowing for something even better:** Try to be as specific as possible while also being broad enough to allow for a little magic. You might surprise yourself!

Here are some examples to help illustrate effective goal setting:

PROFESSIONAL/FINANCIAL:

- I love that my business is thriving, and I get to learn, earn, grow, and contribute.

- I feel secure in my net worth and income and know it will provide an amazing life and continue to grow.

FAMILY/LOVE/RELATIONSHIPS:

- I have deep love in my life, and my partner and I are co-creating an extraordinary relationship.

- I am accepted and celebrated exactly as I am. This relationship gives me what I want and need and is safe, easy and fun.

HEALTH/COMMUNITY/JOY:

- I am in excellent physical shape, with abundant energy.

- I have deep, meaningful friendships that inspire me and support my growth.

- I enjoy life, feel free, and have all the time I need to live fully in the present.

Step 3: Execute: Use OKRs to Improve Outcomes

Goals without execution are worthless. Though goals and objectives are often used interchangeably, they're different. Think of your Freedom Goals as the big picture—the vision, the destination, the thing you're ultimately aiming for. Objectives are the tangible, measurable steps that get you there. One of the most effective methods I've found to translate dreams and goals into reality is the OKRs (objectives and key results) framework. OKRs are made up of two parts:

1. **Objectives** are the ambitious goals that inspire you and others toward a big outcome. An objective is a statement of direction and intent (i.e., where you or your team want to go). Objectives are *not* meant to describe how you will get there.

2. **Key results** are the incremental milestones that measure progress toward the objective. They are usually quantitative but can be qualitative.

These two parts work together: Key results keep us on track as we navigate toward our exciting destination, the objective. We need both parts to know where we're going and how to get there.

Here is an example of an OKR we established with one of our companies:

- **Objective:** Move company from normal (10 percent) to hyper-growth mode (>30 percent).

- **Why does it matter?** Growth sets us up for a bright future with many options.

- **Key result 1:** Velocity growth in top twenty existing accounts above 20 percent.

- **Key result 2:** Add two thousand new customers by August.

- **Key result 3:** Improve margin to above 35 percent for top twenty customers.

Here's an example of one of my personal OKRs:

- **Objective:** I am so happy to have abundant energy and be pain free.

- **Why does it matter?** Having high energy and being pain free are freedom to me.

- **Key result 1:** Work out for a minimum of thirty minutes a day, six days a week.

- **Key result 2:** Yoga or active stretching at least three times per week.

- **Key result 3:** No alcohol Sunday through Thursday. Period.

Each of these will have specific initiatives associated with them, but what's most powerful about OKRs is they give everyone in the organization a common language, framework, and way to regularly track progress.

Step 4: Reinforce Through Multisensory Tools

Reinforce your vision of freedom with multisensory, multi-touch-point tools that keep your goals alive and front of mind. These tools anchor your dreams in your daily life and help align your actions with your aspirations.

- **Freedom binder:** Create a dedicated space to document your goals, progress, and reflections. Include visual elements like photos, affirmations, or written descriptions of your dream life. I had a beachfront property in mine years before we bought our beach house. Now, I have a house in the hills and an old pickup truck in front. This tangible resource serves as a constant reminder of what you're working toward.

- **Visual reminders:** Use a vision board or digital collage filled with images that reflect your goals. Place it somewhere you'll see daily—at home, in your office, or both.

- **Auditory tools:** Curate a playlist of songs that evoke the emotions and energy of your dream life. I now have a "freedom playlist" on Spotify.

- **Supercharge with AI:** I've started using AI to help refine and organize my goals—everything from tracking progress to brainstorming bold new dreams. It's like having a personal assistant, life coach, and strategic advisor all rolled into one (without needing coffee breaks).

- **Share your vision:** Share your aspirations with trusted people who can provide encouragement and accountability. Of course, balance transparency with confidentiality where necessary. Sharing creates healthy pressure and accountability while fostering connection.

By using these multisensory tools and involving others in your journey, you'll stay aligned, motivated, and focused, increasing the likelihood of turning your dreams into reality.

THE TAKEAWAYS
Step 4: Free to Dream

What's the Point?

Dreams are more than wishful thinking; they're the blueprint for building a life of success, wealth, meaning, and freedom. Without dreams, we drift. With them, we rise.

Why Is This Important?

Dreams keep us moving forward. They push us to take risks, grow, and create meaningful lives and businesses. Dreams inspire clarity, focus, and resilience, helping you unlock potential and possibilities you never imagined.

How To: Start Dreaming Bigger

- **Reconnect with old dreams:** Reflect on what once excited you. What dreams have you outgrown, and which ones still light you up?

- **Give yourself permission to dream freely:** Forget limits. Write down what you truly want—without editing or doubting.

- **Visualize, emotionalize, and break it down:** Picture your dream in vivid detail, imagine how you feel, then reverse engineer the steps to get there. Use tools like vision boards, trackers, and goal maps to stay focused and inspired.

Go Deeper

- Books:

  - *The Big Leap* by Gay Hendricks
  - *Dream Big* by Bob Goff

- Tools (markrampolla.co):

  - Full-body-ization
  - Dream Inventory Journal
  - Goal-Setting Blueprint

What's Next?

Dreaming is a key step toward freedom. In Step 5, we'll explore how discipline, habits, and bold action turn visions into reality—and take you further than you thought possible.

FREEDOM TAKES DISCIPLINE

A few years after selling ZICO, I attended a large beverage industry conference. I'd been to this event many times before, initially working hard to get ZICO (and me) noticed. But now, as a VIP, I was invited to attend an exclusive dinner with top industry players: investment bankers, private equity investors, corporate CEOs, and a few ultra-successful entrepreneurs.

I sat beside a serial founder who had at least two major exits under his belt, including one in the alcohol industry. We ordered single malt scotches and, when offered, glasses of cabernet. But by the end of the night, I noticed he'd barely touched his drinks. Meanwhile, I had finished both of mine and was on a second glass of wine. I was intrigued. Given his background in spirits and having more wealth than probably anyone at the table, why was he holding back?

Looking around, I realized that nearly everyone at the table had drunk little or nothing. This was surprising. At most industry gatherings I'd been to up to this point, people had enjoyed a few cocktails or beers before dinner, with wine flowing freely throughout the night, especially when someone else was paying the tab.

After dinner, some old friends waved me over in the hotel lobby and asked me to join them for a drink. Initially, I declined, but one insisted: "Come on, spend some time with the little people." I relented and ordered a round of good tequila, and we dove into old beverage war stories. They peppered me with questions about life after ZICO: Was I traveling the world, enjoying the "dark side" as an investor, or planning a comeback?

At one point, I looked around the bar and noticed something striking—no one from the dinner was there. It suddenly hit me: This was the B-team. The A-team had already gone to bed.

I paid the bill, left a generous tip, said my goodbyes, and headed to my room. As I rode up the elevator, I reflected on the contrast between my two experiences: the disciplined structure of the A-team at dinner and the easygoing camaraderie of the B-team at the bar. Both were enjoyable, but they represented two very different approaches to life, business, and success.

I realized that although I'd been reasonably disciplined while building ZICO, I rarely demonstrated the level of control I saw from these top leaders. Honestly, my version of discipline often involved last-minute sprints and Post-it notes scattered across my desk.

I'd always thought of discipline as something that limited freedom, but what if the opposite was true? What if the freedom I wanted—which included operating among the best in the world and pursuing even bigger goals—required even more discipline?

The realization stung, but it was clear: My next chapter would require a whole other level of discipline—and less tequila.

The Freedom to Choose Discipline

What does discipline—like choosing not to drink—have to do with freedom? At first glance, self-restraint seems to conflict with the bold goal of personal freedom. But here's the irony: True freedom requires discipline. Discipline creates the space to think clearly, grow, and make intentional choices that both allow us to be present and propel us forward toward our goals. The most successful leaders understand that following every impulse isn't freedom; it's being ruled by whim. Without structure, freedom unravels into chaos.

That dinner with the disciplined founder was an eye-opener. It wasn't that he couldn't indulge in more whiskey or stay out late; he simply chose not to. He understood something I was just beginning to grasp: Mastery over small daily decisions leads to mastery over life. His choice wasn't about denying himself but perhaps about preserving his energy and clarity. He had the "freedom" to do whatever he wanted, but he was focused on his intentions, not fleeting indulgences.

Inspired, I began reevaluating my own choices and routines. I questioned whether the habits that had served me while building ZICO still aligned with what I wanted in this next phase of life. I tested everything—diet, sleep, exercise, drinking, work routines—through one lens: Does this bring more energy, clarity, and freedom—or less? It wasn't easy; I quickly learned that changing habits feels less like a makeover and more like untangling a string of Christmas lights.

Discipline isn't just about restraint; it's about generating, managing, and channeling energy where and how you choose. As I made changes to my life, at times, I had so much energy that I risked spinning out of control, chasing projects simply because I had the fuel to do so. I even briefly considered becoming an ultra-runner like Dan—until I remembered I got bored driving one hundred miles, let alone running them.

I had to learn to manage that energy, channeling it intentionally toward what truly mattered. This taught me a critical lesson: Skills, knowledge, and drive are essential, but without sustained energy, they don't translate into meaningful results. And building and maintaining energy take discipline.

But discipline also demands accepting your own unique challenges. You can't do someone else's work or follow their path—and they can't do or follow yours. Others might seem to have it easier in certain ways. They may face struggles you can't imagine. Accept this and let it go. What if the challenges you're facing are exactly what you need to grow into your freedom? This perspective transforms obstacles from barriers into opportunities for growth. It's not about comparing your journey to others' but recognizing that you have a choice in every situation, and each choice is a step closer to or further away from your own liberation.

In the following sections, I'll share the key areas I've found to have the greatest leverage in creating discipline—areas where focused effort brought me the greatest return in terms of energy, clarity, and freedom. While everyone's journey is unique, consider this a starting point. What's hard for me might be a breeze for you, and vice versa. Take stock of the discipline you already have, acknowledge how it has served you, and explore new practices. With greater discipline, you can access more energy, presence, and freedom in your life.

Guidelines for Creating Discipline

Discipline is the foundation of freedom. It's built over time with steady effort and intention. Here are seven steps that can help create the discipline necessary for lasting success and freedom:

1. Acknowledge and celebrate existing discipline.

Begin by recognizing where you're already disciplined. Take pride in the areas where you've succeeded in cultivating positive habits or routines. Reflect on how you built those habits; it's a road map for applying discipline to other areas of your life. I'm learning French, and I take a moment of pride when I do even a ten-minute lesson each day. Even just writing this gets me excited to put on my Audible course!

2. Identify what's not serving you.

Assess your habits through the lens of your future goals. What routines or choices are no longer aligned? Approach this exercise with compassion; whatever you did probably served a purpose at the time. Release judgment, honor the role those habits once played, and let them go to make space for new, intentional practices. I have a group of buddies I've been skiing with for twenty-plus years. I love you fellas, but I've got other priorities this year. Maybe the next!

3. Build positive habits.

Discipline is often the result of small daily habits that compound over time. Start with one area where you desire more freedom—whether in health, work, or personal growth—and focus on one habit to move you forward. James Clear's *Atomic Habits* offers a practical framework:

- **Make it obvious:** Design your environment to make the habit easy to follow. Want to read more? Place a book by your bed.

- **Make it attractive:** Pair the habit with something enjoyable, like listening to audiobooks while exercising.

- **Make it easy:** Start small. Meditate for two minutes, then gradually increase.

- **Make it satisfying:** Reward yourself for each step, acknowledging even small wins. Again, progress is progress.

To break negative habits, reverse these principles: Make them invisible, unattractive, difficult, and unsatisfying. For instance, I used to display my wine and alcohol collection with pride. Now I keep it in the closet.

1. Move toward pain and fear.

Instead of avoiding discomfort, face it head-on. Phil Stutz and Barry Michels's *The Tools* emphasizes the power of confronting pain, as it often sets you free.[13] Start viewing moments of discomfort as opportunities for growth, and lean into them rather than running away.

I once offered to meet with a coinvestor who was particularly angry about losing money after following me into one opportunity. I wasn't exactly excited about it and imagined the worst—anger, blame, and harsh words. But I did it anyway. It wasn't easy sitting there, listening to his frustrations, but it also wasn't as bad as I'd built it up to be. In fact, those conversations turned out to be good for both of us. He got to express how he felt, and I took responsibility for my part and didn't deny or avoid that I got it wrong. I felt much lighter afterward versus staying stuck in regret or resentment.

---

13 Phil Stultz and Barry Michels, *The Tools* (Random House, 2013).

2. What not to do is as important as what to do.

Successful people are highly intentional about what they say yes to—and fiercely protective of their energy. Half of discipline is learning to set boundaries and eliminate activities, meetings, or commitments that drain you or distract from your goals. The mantra "say no to good to leave room for great" helps keep priorities clear.

I've had to learn this lesson the hard way. I get countless requests from early stage entrepreneurs asking for advice. I genuinely want to help, and I feel some guilt when I can't respond to everyone. I used to try to squeeze in as many calls and meetings as I could, thinking I was giving back. But over time, I realized I was really avoiding feeling guilt, and it was leaving me depleted—drained of the energy I needed to focus on the companies we'd already invested in.

By becoming more disciplined about saying no, I've been able to channel my energy more effectively, showing up fully for the commitments that matter most. And I get to learn to feel guilty and do what I want anyway. The guilt passes. Setting boundaries isn't selfish; it's what allows us to make a bigger impact where it counts.

3. Test, track, learn, and integrate.

Adopt a scientific mindset to identify practices that truly serve you. Choose an area—such as sleep—and run a simple experiment, such as avoiding caffeine in the evening. Track the results, and adjust accordingly. Take time to integrate the new habit. This is equally true with most meaningful experiences. You're getting, at most, half the benefit of any experience—a new habit, a trip, a conference—if you rush on to the next. After a big trip or work event, I always block time to write about or just reflect on what the experience meant to me. Experimenting and integrating creates a cycle of growth, turning insights into meaningful, lasting change.

4. Use the Freedom Key.

Consider using the Freedom Key around discipline, and ask yourself:

- *What am I thinking about this area of discipline? Am I sure I'm right?*

- *What am I feeling?*

- *What do I want? Acknowledgment? Control? Security?*

- *Can I let that go?*

This framework helps challenge assumptions and frees you from thoughts or feelings that limit you. For instance, you may feel that you struggle with discipline. The Freedom Key can help you see that, question it, and release it so that you can move forward to create the discipline you want in your life.

High-Leverage Areas of Discipline Bring the Most Freedom

In refining my routines, I found four areas that have the highest impact on my energy, productivity, and freedom: evening and morning routines; consumption; rest, recovery, and play; and core business routines. When I stay consistent in these areas—even 70 percent of the time—I generally feel at peace, energized, and free to pursue my highest goals.

I'll start by saying that I'm no guru when it comes to habits. There are plenty of people who could run circles around me with their color-coded planners, fitness and sleep routines, and meditation streaks. But I'll share what's worked for me—and if nothing else, it might give you a few ideas to borrow (or avoid).

It's a journey of patience, experimentation, and discipline, but the rewards—sustained energy, productivity, and freedom—are well worth it. The science backs it up. According to Charles Duhigg, author of *The Power of Habit*, habits are powerful because they create neurological cravings, leading to a cycle of behavior that is hard to break.[14]

Freedom Today Begins Last Night

The quality of sleep you get shapes your productivity for the next day. Here's what I focus on in my evening routine:

- **Food, drink, and supplements:** I finish my last meal two hours before bed and drink water (and ZICO) throughout the day (aiming for a gallon), finishing my last glass an hour before sleep. Those who knew me years ago may be shocked, but as a rule, I don't drink during the week. If I drink at all (which is rare these days) it's one or two glasses of very good wine on a Friday or Saturday night only. There's always a cost, so it has to be worth it. I also swear by high-quality magnesium supplements.

- **Electronics and light:** Blue light from screens disrupts sleep, so I follow a "digital sunset," turning off screens two hours before bed and dimming lights. I have blackout shades and no TV in my bedroom and keep my phone away from the bed. I travel with a roll of black tape to cover those annoying little lights in hotel rooms.

- **Ditch the pillow:** Switching to a thin rolled towel instead of a pillow virtually eliminated neck pain from my life. Years later, I sometimes still miss pillows, but it's so worth it.

---

14 Charles Duhigg, *The Power of Habit: Why We Do What We Do in Life and Business* (Random House, 2012).

- **Heat, cold, and inversion:** I was never a bath guy. I am now, at least before bed. I sleep best in a cold room and even use the Eight Sleep system to keep my mattress cool. Before bed, I practice inversion by lying back and raising my legs overhead for five to ten minutes.

This routine doesn't guarantee, but dramatically improves, the probability of deep sleep, and I am so much calmer, clearer, more energized, and more present the following day.

Good Morning!

With no kids in my house, I know I have an unfair advantage over those battling cereal spills and missing shoes. But I've always made "me time" a nonnegotiable in the morning—because if I don't start the day right, who knows where it'll end up? Here are a few of my best hacks:

- **Start slow:** I typically wake at 5 or 5:30 a.m. and spend ten to fifteen minutes in a lucid dream state, focusing on gratitude. I often wake up with my mind racing, but I've learned to just laugh and feel grateful for even that. It's pure bliss!

- **Hydrate:** I drink a half liter of water immediately when I wake, followed by 1 liter of ZICO or hot water with lemon, and refill a 1.5-liter bottle with electrolytes to finish before noon.

- **Move naturally:** I do twenty to forty minutes of resistance stretching: back, core, and legs. This is nonnegotiable for me, no matter what's going on or where in the world I am. If I do this, I am pain free. A few days off and for sure something will be out of whack.

- **Meditation:** I meditate for twenty to forty minutes daily. I often add ten minutes to recall situations from the previous day and the emotions I experienced to hone my emotional intelligence. If I'm struggling to "feel," I listen to my sad playlist and watch the emotions (and sometimes tears) start to flow.

- **Intermittent fasting:** Fasting from 8 p.m. until at least noon has been transformative for my energy. I'll have ZICO, coffee, or matcha but nothing else.

- **Sauna and cold plunge:** I usually hit the sauna three times a week, and while my relationship with the cold plunge is somewhere between *love* and *why am I doing this to myself?*, nothing makes me feel more focused and alive than two or three minutes in that icy torture chamber.

Free to Consume (or Not)

It turns out that "you are what you eat" applies to more than just food. If I binge junk—whether it's processed sugar or mindless TV—I feel sluggish and unmotivated. So I try to be mindful about what I take in. Here's how I approach consumption:

- **Real food:** Inspired by Michael Pollan's advice—"Eat real food, not too much, mostly plants"[15]—I stick to minimally processed, nutrient-dense, high-quality foods.

- **Mindful eating:** When I feel hungry or before I sit down to eat, I try to give myself even just a minute of space between the craving and the eating. I chew (which, frankly, I'm not sure I used to really do at all) aiming for thirty times per bite. Once a year, I do a weeklong fast, and I fast most of the day when I travel, never eating on planes.

- **Mindful drinking:** I rarely drink anymore, but I keep a stash of nonalcoholic options on hand to mimic my old habits. At first, I felt guilty about not ordering drinks when I was out— partly because I worried I wasn't being a *good customer.* Now, I let the guilt go, challenge bartenders to create something interesting, and tip like I've just ordered a round of top-shelf martinis. Turns out, they appreciate a fun challenge—and I wake up without regrets.

- **Selective media:** "You are what you eat" applies to mental consumption too. I'm picky about news, avoid most sports, and barely touch social media. Sure, I might miss the latest pop culture trends and couldn't tell you who won the big game—but I'll trade those blind spots for the mental clarity and peace I gain any day. Plus, it's amazing how often people will fill you in on what's going on in the world, whether you ask or not.

- **Healthy indulgence:** I believe in indulging—just intentionally. Whether it's dark chocolate with almond butter, an amazing glass of wine, or a gloriously bad B movie, I let myself enjoy

---

15 Michael Pollan, *In Defense of Food: An Eater's Manifesto* (Penguin Books, 2009).

it fully and slowly. If I take my time and savor it, I'm usually satisfied for a while—though, let's be honest, dark chocolate doesn't stay safe in my pantry for long.

Rest, Recovery, and Play

Entrepreneurs often glorify intensity, but unchecked hustle can backfire. I learned that balancing focus with intentional rest boosts productivity and well-being. Here's my approach:

- **Regular breaks:** Short breaks or even naps during the day prevent burnout and keep me fresh. I had a sign outside my ZICO office saying, "Good things come to those who nap." Thomas Edison was a master of the catnap; maybe that's how he kept the bright ideas flowing.

- **Scheduled downtime:** I rarely work nights or weekends. Sure, I still feel a twinge of guilt about it—like my laptop is silently judging me—but I've discovered an undeniable truth: The more I embrace my inner sloth over the weekend, the more I'm a productivity ninja on Monday.

- **Play:** It's not just for kids! I'm amazed how many entrepreneurs have, well, no life. When asked for his success advice, shipping magnate Aristotle Onassis allegedly said, "Get a tan."

Discipline in Business Routines

When my personal life is in alignment (following most of what I previously mentioned), maintaining discipline in business routines becomes much easier. These routines keep my work life focused, improve my energy, and enhance my sense of freedom:

- **Ferocious calendaring:** Weekly, I review every meeting and event in advance, asking, *Is this how I really want to spend my time?* Anything unnecessary gets cut.

- **Energy audit:** I regularly conduct an energy audit on up coming meetings, asking myself, *is this an energy up or down?* I cancel anything that is down. Energy, not time, is our most valuable resource. Protect it carefully.

- Additonally, your goals change over time, whereas your values—which many of us rarely define or use as guides for our goals—may be more enduring.

- **OKR reviews:** Our firm sets annual OKRs, and I set personal ones too. We review them monthly as a team, and I check mine weekly to identify top initiatives. Each day, I review them before diving into tasks.

- **First things first:** Each day, I prioritize one or two high-focus tasks and tackle them during pre-blocked time. Progress on even one important task boosts my energy.

- **Speak less, ask more:** I strive to speak less and ask more questions. It empowers others, conserves my energy, and often leads to better outcomes.

- **Don't be a slave to email:** I batch process emails two or three times a day. Instant responses may make you feel productive in the moment, but they often hijack your focus and train both you and everyone around you to value urgency over structured work driven by importance.

- **Thought time:** I dedicate three to four hours a week for uninterrupted reading, reflection, and brainstorming. No electronics—just a pen and paper. This fuels creativity and freedom, and many of my best ideas emerge here.

- **Blind spot detector**: I have a sign next to my desk I look at whenever I feel I have most things under control. It reads, "What am I avoiding, suppressing, ignoring, denying, minimizing, or rationalizing?"—because I know now, there's *always* something. It's usually lurking just out of sight, like that pile of mail I keep pretending doesn't exist. Spotting it early keeps me grounded—and saves me from bigger messes later.

- **AI as a strategic assistant**: I've begun using AI as a sort of "productivity partner," helping me conduct research, better organize and access my own past writings, and generate visual images as tools and reminders for my freedom. It's a powerful tool that can limit or expand one's freedom—the choice is yours!

The Paradox of Freedom

The paradox of freedom is that it isn't about limitless choices or escaping responsibilities; it's about making choices that serve your highest self and your highest goals. Freedom requires discipline: the discipline to know what truly matters to you and to pursue it with intention. Without discipline, freedom is fragile, lost in the chaos of impulses and distractions. But with discipline, freedom becomes a deep-rooted way of being. Discipline fuels energy, clarity, and, alignment, creating the foundation for lasting success and freedom.

As I learned from that dinner with the A-team, success doesn't mean achieving everything and resting in endless freedom. It comes from mastering the discipline to grow, evolve, and stay aligned with your purpose.

When I look at myself critically, I often fall short of much of what I've written above. But then I usually laugh, have compassion for myself, and know that I tend to hold the highest standards and toughest criticism for myself! When I can practice these principles, even only on occasion, I pass the ultimate test: I feel more calm, present, and free. Remember to give yourself patience and compassion. Building new habits takes time, and entrepreneurs excel at measuring themselves and finding room for improvement. That's OK. See it, accept it, release it, and return to freedom.

Discipline isn't about perfection; it's about intention and awareness. Discipline is power. By creating routines that serve your highest self, you set the stage not only for more success, greater meaning, and more wealth but for a life of joy, purpose, and sustained freedom. Embrace the process, and let discipline guide you to the freedom you seek.

SIGN ON MY WALL: All work and no play is no fun at all
(Mark Rampolla, wannabe artist)

FREEDOM TOOL: Energy Audit

Our energy fuels our freedom. When we're energized, we're more focused, more creative, and able to pursue what matters most. An energy audit helps you maximize positive energy and build a life with more freedom by managing your commitments intentionally.

Step 1: Look Back

Review your calendar for the past week. Rate each meeting as either "energy up" or "energy down."

- **Energy up:** You felt engaged and more energized after the meeting—these are the ones you want more of.

- **Energy Down:** You left drained or disengaged—these are the ones you'd prefer to avoid.

Calculate your ratio of "energy up" to "energy down." Set this as a baseline and repeat weekly, aiming to increase the proportion of energizing commitments. A goal of 70 percent "energy up" is a solid benchmark, recognizing that not every meeting will be a perfect fit.

Step 2: Look Forward

Evaluate your meetings for the coming week. Cancel at least one "energy down" meeting right now. Resist the urge to justify your decision; simply observe how it feels to prioritize your own energy.

Repeat this process each week. By intentionally clearing space for "energy up" activities, you'll notice a shift toward more focus, satisfaction, and freedom. Even small changes can create a cycle of positive momentum that fuels both personal fulfillment and productivity.

THE TAKEAWAYS
Step 5: Freedom Takes Discipline

What's the Point?

Freedom takes discipline. Structure and consistency create the foundation for lasting success, allowing you to turn dreams into reality and maintain your freedom.

Why Is This Important?

Discipline is the bridge between dreaming and achieving. Without it, dreams fall apart. True freedom requires daily habits, clear priorities, and the ability to say no to distractions so you can say yes to what moves you forward. Discipline isn't restrictive; it's power.

How To: Build Discipline That Fuels Freedom

- **Focus on priorities:** Define your top goals, and break them into daily, weekly, and monthly actions. Track progress, and adjust as needed.

- **Create systems and habits:** Use tools like time-blocking, checklists, and routines to stay organized and accountable.

- **Practice saying no:** Protect your time and energy by eliminating distractions and setting boundaries. Focus on what aligns with your vision.

Go Deeper

- **Books:**
  - *Atomic Habits* by James Clear
  - *Essentialism* by Greg McKeown
- **Tools (markrampolla.co):**
  - Full Body Yes
  - Energy Audit
  - Weekly Freedom and Success Habits

What's Next?

Discipline creates the foundation for freedom, but freedom isn't static; it demands growth and adaptability. Sustaining it means being willing to change what no longer serves you. In Step 6, we'll explore how embracing change can unlock even greater freedom.

FREE TO CHANGE

We had gathered our team of seven at Terranea resort outside of Los Angeles for an annual two-day off-site meeting to discuss our firm's strategy and plans for the following year.

As I walked into the conference room—earlier than our start time—I saw Nicole, Julianne, and Cessna scrambling frantically, grabbing snacks and beverages from the table. They looked surprised and anxious when I entered.

"What, are you taking the good ones for yourselves?" I joked.

Their faces froze with fear. I knew something more serious was in play. "What's going on? Is everything all right?"

They all looked at one another. Julianne, recently promoted to vice president—the most senior of the three—said sheepishly, "Well, we just realized one of the snacks has honey in it. We're so sorry. We know that honey is not technically vegan, so we just decided to get rid of everything until we could inspect them all."

I tried to make light of the matter: "I won't tell my bee-loving friends, I promise." But I realized from their reaction they were taking this very seriously.

"We're just trying to make sure everything we do is vegan," Nicole added. "I mean, isn't that in keeping with our values as a firm?"

"OK, I can see that. But are you doing this for yourselves or for someone else?" I asked.

They looked at each other again and replied in unison, "Well, for you and the other partners."

"None of us are hardcore vegan," Cessna added. "We all eat mostly plants, but we just assumed this is what you wanted. I mean, it's in our name."

I told them that while partners TK and Kevin were strictly vegan, Dan and I were not. I said that none of us were so dogmatic that we wanted to dictate how they lived their lives.

After a pause, I said, "Look, this clearly warrants a bigger discussion, but I promise you this: You are free to eat what you want, when you want. Julianne, you're pregnant; feed yourself and your baby what you think you need! Put all the snacks out. Everyone can read the labels and choose what they want."

They looked relieved, but I knew there was a bigger issue at hand.

Later, I pulled Dan aside, told him what happened, and said, "We need to talk."

The Power of Plants

The idea for what would become PowerPlant Ventures was born as a vision of TK Pillan and Kevin Boylan. They were co-founders of Veggie Grill, the largest plant-based restaurant chain in the country—twenty-plus outlets at the time and growing.

TK was of Indian descent. His parents were vegan, but he grew up outside of Boston eating burgers and playing basketball and baseball and went into tech. Kevin was all finance, having worked for Michael Milken at Drexel Burnham for a decade.

TK became vegan for ethical reasons, Kevin for health reasons. Between the two, they saw the opportunity to create a plant-based restaurant chain accessible to all—no having to rub the Buddha's belly, chant mantras, or eat tasteless brown rice sitting on the floor. Just healthy, delicious, and convenient food that happened to be plant-based.

Their timing was perfect. Veganism was going mainstream.

I became a regular Veggie Grill customer and, after selling ZICO, invested in the company. TK and Kevin approached me about joining them in starting a venture fund to invest in this emerging space. I wasn't vegan but was moving more and more plant-based at the time—mainly for environmental reasons, and I also saw the trend in the market and knew they were on to something.

We launched PowerPlant Ventures in 2015 with a first $42 million fund. We were strong out of the gate, with investments in Thrive Market, Appel Sciences, Ripple Milk, and Beyond Meat, which became the darling of the entire natural food industry with a $3.8 billion initial public offering in 2019. For a moment, we felt like geniuses—and there were some who agreed.

Plants Taking Over the World

It looked like the beginning of a revolution in food. Beyond Meat's IPO had attracted global attention. There was talk about plant-based food becoming a trillion-dollar market. This attracted more and better entrepreneurs to the space. As one Stanford professor told us, "I'm not sure what's happening, but the best students all used to go into tech. Now more and more are going into food, and it's all plant-based."

The buzz also attracted capital. Just about every major venture firm had a person or small team looking at food tech. Soon, there were also multiple funds with a similar focus to ours. Some were backed by vegan billionaires and were so focused on changing the world that they seemed to care little about making money. Middle Eastern sovereign wealth funds also poured money into the space, hoping it might help them with food security concerns.

Lots of capital chasing a limited number of companies meant valuations went sky-high. Some ideas, like cellular meat, would take hundreds of millions of dollars and a decade to become even remotely price competitive with meat. We didn't have the capital—or the patience—to play that game. Plus, the meat industry fought back hard, and some groups questioned the health credentials of products like Beyond Meat. Let's just say not everyone was ready to trade in their burgers and steaks.

Beyond Meat's founder, Ethan Brown, devised a strategy to go head-to-head with meat: Offer consumers a viable alternative with the Beyond Burger, and move it out of the vegan section of supermarkets and into the meat aisle. Retailers eventually got behind the strategy, and velocity went through the roof—proof that even die-hard carnivores could be tempted if the burger didn't come with a side of kale chips and judgment.

Not everyone was thrilled—particularly a militant group labeled the Vegan Mafia. Ethan got hate mail from some of them who didn't want to set foot in the meat aisle, apparently more concerned about their own views—or how they might look to others—than truly scaling the movement. One vegan company founder forbade employees from eating any animal-based food while at work. Soon, there was infighting among the various vegan tribes.

Still, we remained bullish. As we continued to gear up to capitalize on this momentum, we realized we needed another partner with deeper investing experience. Enter Dan Gluck. Dan had managed a billion-dollar portfolio for a prominent hedge fund in New York. He had been an angel investor in ZICO some years earlier. He had also cofounded a nutrition bar business called Health Warrior, which he had sold to Pepsi. While not vegan, he, like me, was interested in plant-based food for health and wellness as well as climate impact and saw the potential of building a food-centric investment firm.

Dan joined as our fourth partner, with he and I assuming the roles of comanaging partners, and we successfully raised a second fund of $167 million. We invested that fund following the same strategy, focusing on early stage plant-based companies. But as we started to chart a path for our future, we began to have questions.

Dan had been digging into the numbers and came to a tough conclusion: It would be really hard, if not impossible, to get the kind of returns we hoped for with an early-stage consumer-products venture fund. The reality was that a lot of early stage investments would fail, and while we might get a few big wins—maybe even a ten-times return on one or two—the numbers still didn't add up.

In tech, venture funds could sometimes hit massive wins—returns of fifty or greater times on a single investment—which could offset the losses on others. But in consumer products, those kinds of home runs are extremely rare. With an appropriate number of failures still baked into the model, it was tough to make the math work when focusing only on early stage consumer brands.

As we began to consider raising a third fund, we started to wonder: Was our current approach too risky? Was our focus on early stage and only plant-based companies too narrow? Should we stick to our knitting, leverage our reputation and expertise, and maintain our discipline?

Or should we consider a dramatic pivot, shifting the entire firm to expand beyond plant-based and focus on investing in companies at the growth stage instead of venture?

If we moved into growth, that would mean we needed an entirely new team, operating advisors, and support network. It would be a very different level of diligence to underwrite investing $10–$20 million into a company already doing $20–$100 million in revenue versus investing a few million into a true start-up. Were we willing to throw away what seemed to be working for some unknown future?

Dan and I went on a three-day hike scaling the glacier-capped Mount Baker in Washington state to discuss this. Crampons strapped to our boots, we trudged over crevasses, led by a young female guide who absolutely kicked our asses—and barely broke a sweat doing it. As we gasped for air and questioned our professional and life choices, we also gave ourselves the freedom to ask bigger questions: If we were starting fresh, what would we do? Would we even start an investment firm—or something entirely different? Would we do it alone, with others, or together? We gave ourselves and each other the freedom to at least explore whatever scenarios we wanted.

We both decided we wanted to work together and that we wanted to continue as an investment firm. We reminded ourselves that we shared a deep commitment to health and wellness, sustainability, and personal development. We wanted those to be core to whatever we did. Other than that, we were open. We also decided plant-based was a component but wasn't core to who we were. It was a tactic that we would continue to employ, not an overarching strategy. We decided we were willing to invest beyond just plant-based, elevating health and wellness and sustainability as more important principles. That was a big risk. What would our other partners think? Our team? Our investors? What would the market think? We had worked so hard to build our reputation—and it was literally in our name!

Although we had some fear, we left the mountain determined. We were not sure what the path forward was, but we knew we didn't want more of the same. We wanted to—needed to—change.

Over the following months, we dove deep into refining and pressure testing this new strategy. Where and how we would invest. What team we would need. How we would need to change as leaders. How we would communicate this change to our network and the market. We decided to rename the firm and, after a thorough process, landed on GroundForce Capital. We would invest in high-potential growth stage companies seeking to improve the health and longevity of people and the planet. It was a bold pivot.

"What Took You So Long?"

We knew this new strategy would require a completely new team. We loved our existing group, but their background and experience were geared to venture. We knew we needed to surround ourselves with a team that had extensive experience in investment banking, growth, private equity, and institutional capital management.

It's amazing how, sometimes, when you set an intention and go all in, things just fall into place.

Julianne was recruited by a top venture firm in New York. Cessna moved to a great early stage consumer fund in San Francisco. Nicole became a personal coach. We wished them all well. TK and Kevin supported our change in strategy but decided to gradually move into more advisory roles at the firm so they could pursue interests more aligned with their values.

Dan and I went on to build an incredible team—now thirteen strong—made up of passionate, driven, and experienced professionals. We recruited a suite of world-class operating advisors to support us and our companies. We believe our team can hold its own against firms twice our size. While we all share a commitment to health, wellness, sustainability, and personal growth, everyone's free to eat however they choose.

We raised $330 million in our next fund. The first few investments happened to be plant-based, but we were determined to prove—to ourselves and the world—that we were no longer just "the plant-based firm." We were GroundForce Capital . . . we just hadn't told anyone yet. It felt a bit like getting a cool new haircut and waiting for the perfect moment to debut it. We wanted to make the announcement alongside the right new investment—something bold, different, and definitely not made of tofu.

We found it in Bobbie Baby Formula.

Bobbie was founded in 2018 by Laura Modi and Sarah Hardy, both former Airbnb executives who, as working moms, wanted access to organic infant formula for their babies—but it wasn't available in the US due to complex and archaic regulations. They were also horrified by the stigma so many women faced when choosing to feed their babies formula. Determined to change that, they started Bobbie to "help every parent feel supported in their feeding journey—breast, bottle, or both."

It was a huge opportunity—a $6 billion market dominated by giants like Abbott Labs and Mead Johnson. Thanks to a connection through a major investor in our third fund, we were introduced to Laura.

As PowerPlant, we wouldn't have even had a shot at this opportunity. Bobbie was and remains dairy-based and was looking to raise

$75 million to acquire a competitor and enable self-manufacturing. Just a year earlier, no one—including us—would have given us a second thought for this opportunity. It didn't fit our plant-based focus, and the deal would have been too big for our earlier funds.

But now, with a broader strategy, a larger fund, and a stronger team, we had a real chance. The only problem? Bobbie was one of the hottest companies in the entire consumer market at the time. We knew we'd be up against leading multibillion-dollar private equity firms. The question wasn't just whether we could compete but whether we could actually win.

There's only one way we would find out: Go all in. And we did. We worked around the clock for weeks preparing a compelling offer and showing Laura and Sarah we were the partners to choose.

We won the deal! We led a $75 million round with a $35 million investment from our fund.

This one investment was almost as big as our first fund.

Simultaneously, with our investment in Bobbie, we announced to the world we were now GroundForce Capital.

When we talked with one major investor about our new name and strategy change, his response came down to one comment: "What took you so long?" I guess he wasn't as emotionally attached to the plant-based label—or the kale smoothies—as we had been.

Free to Change

The entrepreneurial journey, like life, is anything but a smooth, straight path. It's a winding route filled with unexpected turns, bumps, and detours—a thrilling yet unpredictable adventure where the only certainty is uncertainty.

Challenges are inevitable. Some may be minor speed bumps,

while others feel like insurmountable mountains. You'll face forks in the road, feel overwhelmed by options, or be tempted by shiny distractions. At times, you might feel lost, like you're running in circles or stuck in a dead end. Even when you see the light at the end of the tunnel, it can seem to shift out of reach.

Conventional wisdom urges entrepreneurs to persist: *Never quit. Stay the course. Keep pushing forward.* We admire stories of resilience—overcoming, outsmarting, or bulldozing through obstacles. Freedom allows for this. But true freedom also means giving yourself permission to pause, reflect, change direction, or even stop entirely.

These challenges are not only professional; they're personal, too—related to family, health, or life itself. Each stumble, detour, or obstacle provides insights into who you are, what you value, and what you no longer need to do or prove.

Reflection is key. By examining your journey, setbacks, and milestones, you can recommit to your mission with clarity, or pivot entirely. Sometimes, the best decision is to stop and reassess. As the proverb goes, "When you find yourself in a hole, stop digging."

Outcomes are never guaranteed. Every challenge is an opportunity to discover more about yourself and your freedom. The best we can do is constantly be aware of where and how we compromise our freedom; make the best decision we can in any situation, freely; observe what happens; and adapt. This is the path to true freedom: meeting challenges head-on, learning from them, and emerging stronger.

So stay free to change—no matter how committed you think you should be.

FREEDOM TOOL: Return to Freedom

When you find yourself at a crossroads, inflection point, or place of indecision, pause and appreciate it. These moments are incredible opportunities to reflect, assess, and decide whether to keep going, change direction, or stop altogether. Sometimes the decision is clear; other times, it will emerge naturally over time. Sometimes, the best decision is no decision at all and to give yourself the time and space to see what happens.

Here's a tool to help you navigate these moments and move forward with greater freedom, regardless of the decision you make.

Where Am I?

A Diné shaman once shared that in his culture, before making any big decision, the key question they asked is, *Where are we?* Grounding yourself in your current situation is invaluable. Pause and reflect: *What's really going on? Where am I on this journey?* Assess your progress, challenges, and opportunities without shame, blame, or judgment.

Acknowledge what you've accomplished and accept where you are—even if it's not where you hoped to be. Sometimes, what feels like a problem isn't one at all. Ask yourself: *What if this is exactly what I needed?*

Dan and I took months to consider, debate, and observe and finally accepted we were at a crossroads. That alone was freeing and a critical step in the process before we went any further. Start with *where*. Like we mentioned before: location, location, location.

How Did I Get Here?

Ask with genuine curiosity, *How did I create this? What choices, assumptions, or decisions led me here?* Examine your motivations, assumptions, and even fantasies. Assume everyone, including yourself, acted with the best intentions. Reflect without judgment, prioritizing learning over blame or guilt. The goal is to learn and grow, not to assign fault.

Dan and I understood and accepted the past choices we had made, most of them before Dan even joined the firm. We both accepted those decisions were made with the best intention, given the available information at the time. Knowing and respecting our history helped us chart the path we really wanted.

Winston Churchill is often paraphrased as saying, "Those who fail to learn from history are doomed to repeat it."

Free to Recommit or Not

Now that you know where you are and how you got here, ask yourself the tough question: *Do I really want to continue?*

Revisit your goals. Are they still true to your values and passions, or are they driven by fear, obligation, or momentum? Reflect on your role: Do you want to continue as is, or is it time to shift, create space for others, or explore new challenges?

Consider your commitment. Are you truly all in? Freedom means making deliberate choices—even when those choices have real consequences.

Dan and I decided to recommit—to each other and to building an investment firm. But we also chose not to limit ourselves to plant-based investments alone. There's real power in what some call *re-recruitment*—checking in with yourself, your team, and your partners to reaffirm your purpose.

That is now something we do every year. We ask ourselves, each other, and our team, "Do you still want to be on this journey?" Getting everyone's buy-in up front helps avoid the *would have, could have, should have* conversations later. It's basically our version of *speak now or forever hold your peace*—just with fewer tuxedos and less champagne.

Free to Reimagine

Before you proceed, check in again. Does anything need to change? If so, what and how? How could you completely rethink or redesign your business model (or life model) to avoid or minimize this problem or challenge in the future? To get more of what you want and less of what you don't? Is there a way to elevate the solution so you solve it once and for all? How can you make yourself, your business, and your team even more powerful and resilient?

Return to Freedom

If you decide to move forward, do so freely—renewed, energized, and armed with lessons to guide you. But before you do, ask yourself, *Can I do this with even more ease?*

Entrepreneurs tend to dive back in even harder, stronger, faster after a crisis or tough situation. Sometimes, that's the right move. But can you consider doing so with just a little less attachment? A little more ease? Write down what you learned; let this serve as your compass in uncertain times.

When you recommit, do so with clarity, passion, and a deep sense of purpose. This is your return to freedom.

In addition to setting a new direction, Dan and I expanded our vision—to build a multibillion-dollar asset management firm known for improving the health and wellness of people and the planet, all while fostering the best culture in finance. We also asked ourselves, *How can we do that with more ease?* We're still figuring that part out, but the question has us more excited than ever.

THE TAKEAWAYS
Step 6: Free to Change

What's the Point?

Being free to change allows you to shed what no longer serves you, evolve into who you're meant to be, and get more of what you want.

Why Is This Important?

Staying stuck in old patterns, beliefs, or roles can stifle progress and keep you from reaching your potential. The most successful people continually evaluate what's working and what's not and adjust to stay aligned with their goals and values.

How To: Embrace Change and Pivot with Purpose

- **Evaluate what's working:** Regularly review your habits, systems, and relationships. Ask, *Does this still serve me? What needs to shift?*

- **Take small strategic risks:** Start experimenting with small adjustments to test new approaches before making big leaps.

- **Reframe setbacks as opportunities:** View failures as feedback and lessons, not dead ends. Each pivot brings you closer to clarity and success.

Go Deeper

- **Books:**

  - *The Art of Possibility* by Rosamund Stone Zander and Benjamin Zander

- **Tools (markrampolla.co):**

  - Return to Freedom
  - Stop, Start, Continue

What's Next?

Embracing change opens the door to growth, but true freedom is best shared. In Step 7, we'll explore how shared freedom, built on trust and collaboration, can expand possibilities and take you further than you could go alone.

SHARED FREEDOM

After seven years on the PowerPlant to GroundForce Capital journey, the exhaustion I felt was undeniable. I had managed to remain engaged and present, but the weight was building. Raising capital for our various funds and companies, finding and vetting new investment opportunities, sitting on boards, diving in to help companies, and managing the firm were taking their toll.

Friends had initially painted a glamorous picture: *The people I know who run funds have a great life—low stress, summers off, a balanced schedule.* Yet here I was, wondering when I'd experience any of those perks. Instead, I felt like I'd accidentally joined an Ironman—only with more spreadsheets and fewer medals at the finish line.

There was a period where I held nine board seats, often as chairman, each demanding its own time, attention, focus, and decision-making. I even stepped in as interim CEO for two companies. For a guy who has wrestled with ADHD his whole life, it was a relentless juggling act.

Despite my earlier successes, it felt like my learning curve was vertical; there's a reason finance attracts some of the smartest, most driven minds. I'd run a number of companies before, but here, I found myself tested in a completely new way, diving headfirst into a field that felt like it demanded every ounce of focus, energy, and discipline I had—plus a few ounces I didn't.

Managing partners in finance typically come up through decades in investment banking and private equity, honing a grueling level of focus through hundred-hour work weeks, running complex financial models, doing weeks or months of due diligence on companies, and then going even deeper with financial analysis—all the while honing their skills and getting so-called deal reps. At thirty years old, they become trusted partners of CEOs and CFOs twice their ages and sit on boards of companies with more EBITDA (earnings before interest, tax, depreciation, and amortization: a proxy for cash flow, the lifeblood of any company) than the revenue of most companies I had run.

I realized why so few founders successfully transition to institutional investment: It requires a special level of focus, attention, and discipline. And while I'd done a decent job to date, I felt stretched as our third fund brought us into the league of some of the most sophisticated investors on the planet—where impostor syndrome doesn't just whisper; it hires a marching band.

Layered atop these professional demands were intense personal challenges. I'd lost both parents within consecutive years, which left me reeling. The disorganized financials my father had left created distance and complexity among me and my five siblings for the first time in our lives—or perhaps brought to the surface what had been unspoken for years.

My marriage had ended, and I was navigating an emotional divorce while trying to redefine what family meant to the four of us going forward. I moved out of the home I loved and into a nomadic existence of short-term rentals. At one point, I even spent a few nights sleeping in my Tesla between Airbnbs—not expecting any pity, I promise, but it did drive home a not-so-subtle sense of impermanence.

Though we had a nice windfall from selling ZICO, that was a decade ago. I had managed to grow our nest egg, but it was now heavily invested in start-ups, our own funds, and other assets, and it would now all be divided with Maura.

For the first few years at PowerPlant, my income was smaller than at almost any time in my career. It improved after we raised our third fund, our first under the new name, GroundForce Capital, but I now had to factor in the high cost of divorce. On top of that, Dan and I had to make substantial capital commitments for each new fund.

By nearly any measure, I was still wealthy and had a high income, but let's just say the big mountain house I had dreamed of wasn't in the cards anytime soon. Poor me!

Bear in mind, investment firms aren't structured like a start-up, where you work like mad for ten years, hoping for a big payday at the end. With investment firms, success is built incrementally, measured in decades, not years. It takes at least five years per fund before you even know if your strategy will bear fruit, and each typically requires a ten-year commitment.

We were only a few years into our new fund, but it had been about seven years since starting the firm. I was in familiar territory. There it was again, the "seven-year itch" that had shown up in nearly every chapter of my career. I'd spent seven years at International Paper before founding ZICO. I stayed with ZICO for nine years, though by year seven, I was already getting restless. Apparently, I had a nagging seven-year professional itch I just couldn't seem to scratch.

But this time, the stakes felt different. I was over fifty, staring down some fundamental questions: What did I really want now? Was it time to walk away and start something else, or was there a way to transform this life I'd built into something that gave me the freedom I really wanted?

In giving myself the liberty to explore these questions, I came to a revelation: What if I could create exactly what I wanted within and through GroundForce? What if the freedom I was seeking wasn't found by leaving but by reshaping my experience right here? And then the pivotal question surfaced: Why not try to cocreate a new vision of freedom with my partner, Dan?

The Emergence of True Partnership

When I reflected on my track record as a solo investor before Power-Plant, I saw both wins and losses. Some of that was inevitable, but I now better recognized a few of my own blind spots. I could quickly weed out obviously bad investment opportunities, but like most entrepreneurs, I often saw potential where more seasoned investors saw gaps. I lacked the discipline to discern between possibility and reality.

Looking back, I also didn't have a clear, disciplined investment strategy—no tight portfolio construction, thorough diligence process, or other systems professional investors live and die by. Going solo may have been efficient, but it wasn't the best or most fulfilling way forward.

When TK, Kevin, and I started PowerPlant in 2015, we built an investment strategy and processes that worked well for our first $42 million fund. But by 2017, as we set our sights on raising a second fund of $100 million or more, we realized we needed even greater discipline and structure. We were self-aware enough to know that institutional investment expertise wasn't our strongest skill set—and that to scale successfully, we needed to bring in another partner with deeper experience in that world.

From the outset, we had agreed to do whatever it took (consistent with our values) to build a successful firm—even if that meant stepping aside. We'd all seen what happens when founders refuse to let go, and we didn't want to be those guys. I even wondered if I'd be the one to step aside—I wasn't exactly the natural pick to run an institutional investment firm.

But how do you recruit a partner? It would not be like hiring an employee; it's more like getting married, but with fewer romantic dinners and more spreadsheets. So I surrendered, gave it space, and trusted that the right person was already in our orbit. I just needed to open myself to see them emerge.

A few weeks later, I ran into Dan and his wife, Mika, at a trade show. We caught up, and when he asked how things were going at PowerPlant, I admitted it was harder than I expected. He mentioned he was thinking about starting an investment firm himself, and I told him he absolutely should—he had a stronger background for it than I did. That was the end of it—or so I thought.

The next morning, I snapped awake at 5 a.m. with one thought: *It's Dan!* I contained my excitement until 6 a.m. and texted him. He responded immediately. When I asked if he'd consider joining us, he said he would . . . consider it.

One of the things I've grown to love about Dan is that he doesn't make rash decisions. Over the next six months, he reviewed our portfolio, spent time with the other partners and me, and made sure we were aligned on values, strategy, and management style before committing. Honestly, it was like watching someone date us before deciding to move in—and thankfully, we passed the test.

When Dan officially joined and we became comanaging partners, I quickly saw how transformative a true partnership could be. Dan didn't just complement my skills; he challenged me to grow in ways I wouldn't have on my own. He became a sounding board, helping me refine ideas and stay in my "zone of genius." He provided structure where I often lacked it. I played a similarly important but different role for him: helping him cultivate his intuition, see more creative possibilities, experiment more, and take everything a little less seriously.

What surprised me most was how much freedom I gained by letting go of the need to do it all myself. I've always thrived as a lone wolf; it served me well—until it didn't. This partnership taught me that even lone wolves need the pack sometimes. Or at least someone to remind them not to chase every squirrel.

We Bond Through Vulnerability

After we raised our first $330 million fund as GroundForce Capital, I finally decided it was time to share my "seven-year itch" struggle with Dan. By this point, we had been doing coaching—both individually and collectively—for over a year. When I first suggested we get coaching, Dan scoffed: "I don't think we really need that. It's going to be expensive, and will we really get an ROI out of it?" Spoken like a true hedge fund manager.

I replied, "Dan, as your partner, I'm asking. Please, trust me on this."

After the first session, he was hooked. He went deep—deeper than I expected—and the work quickly strengthened our relationship. Over the next six months, we committed fully to completely rebuilding the way we worked together, from the bottom up.

Weekly individual coaching sessions, plus joint sessions twice a month, gave us a shared language to recognize where we were stuck and how to move forward.

One technique we practiced was called "clearing"—a structured way to talk through something that triggered us. Early on, our coach told us, "You've been working together for a few years. It'll take six months to clear everything from the past."

We laughed and said, "We'll do it in two weeks."

We were wrong. It took months.

Old comments. Minor injuries. Assumptions. Unsaid frustrations that had quietly built into resentment. Slowly, we chipped away at them. With each clearing, we saw the power of deep connection and how fluid our communication was becoming.

One day, during a coaching session, I took a deep breath, followed the protocol, and said, "Dan, are you open for a clearing? And it's a big one."

He paused, exhaled, and nodded.

I laid it all out—the exhaustion, the self-doubt, the fears. Then I said:

"I can't keep going at this pace. Well, I could, but I don't want to—and I don't think it's best for me or the firm. I need a break. I want to take a three-month working sabbatical. I'm afraid of how you might respond. I'm afraid of how it'll be perceived: Will I be taken seriously as an investor? What would our investors say? Our companies? Am I too needy? Is it a sign of weakness? What if you and the team realize you don't need me? I also don't know how we'd pull it off. How will it work? Are there legal issues? How will I stay up to speed on my companies? How do we manage the investment committee and other functions?

"I'm worried about all of that.

"But I want it. I need it. And I believe you should have one too. In fact, I think we should turn this into a firm policy. If we can figure this out—and I can take a working sabbatical every so often—then I want to do this job and work with you until I'm in my eighties . . . or longer!"

I exhaled. It was out.

Dan took a deep breath and asked a few questions, and—shockingly—I sensed no resistance. No judgment. Instead, he leaned back, exhaled again, and said, "You have no idea how much I want that for you. And I want it for me, too. I'm afraid of all the same things—and maybe more—but I think we should try to figure it out. And who knows? Maybe it's the best thing for all of us."

The relief was immediate. I wasn't alone. We were both wrestling with similar desire and the same fears—how our absence might be perceived by investors and our team. Would we look irresponsible or weak?

But instead of avoiding it, we leaned in. This was a new possibility of freedom—not just for us, but for the future of GroundForce.

This moment demonstrated the power of a clearing. It worked because we had already cleared a hundred little things over the past year (again, the power of "atomic" habits). That process built the trust we needed to navigate a conversation this big. Good communication doesn't just happen; it's a skill, a habit, that takes time, effort, and intention to cocreate. We had done that work.

What followed were a series of conversations that brought us closer than ever. We brainstormed, and one of our advisors, Andre, helped us look at sabbatical models from top-tier companies including Google, Nike, and Mars. We agreed I would take the first working sabbatical—a structured three-month period living and working from Italy. I'd stay engaged with the companies I covered and available for regular check-ins and key decisions, but give myself enough freedom to rest and reset without abandoning my responsibilities.

In my absence, Dan would lead the firm, and we'd give the team an opportunity to step up and grow in their roles. At the same time, we established systems and routines to make working sabbaticals sustainable—for ourselves, our companies, and our team.

It wasn't just a break—it was a shift in how we defined freedom, leadership, and longevity.

The Transformation of GroundForce

Before I even left for Italy, something remarkable started to unfold at the firm. By sharing this plan with the team, we created space for open dialogue. There were fears and questions but also excitement. We created space for all of it, and everyone had the opportunity to "clear." Then, the team quickly began to get to work. We streamlined our processes, from investment committees to company reviews, aiming for crisp, efficient routines. We defined where decision-making could be delegated and where Dan and I would retain decision rights. Dan took the reins with his unique leadership style, and team members stepped up in ways neither of us had anticipated.

Logan, a new associate who'd assisted me on several companies, began working more directly with founders and CEOs. The results were impressive; he enjoyed the responsibility, the founders valued his input, and I was kept in the loop on key points. During my three-month working sabbatical, I experienced a much-needed reset, and created space for strategic thinking about the future of the firm that I just wasn't doing before. When I returned, GroundForce had transformed. Meetings became more efficient, discussions sharper and more focused—practices we maintain today. Team members who once relied on me found their own strengths and assumed greater roles, with Logan taking his first board seat and eventually earning a promotion to vice president.

While I delegated much of the day-to-day, there were areas I kept close, such as advising the CEO of Vive on a potential sale to Suja Juice. I knew this was one deal that required my direct involvement, and even from Sicily, I had the space to be fully engaged. I thoroughly enjoyed working through the complexities with Vive's CEO, guiding the strategy and ultimately helping to consummate the deal from across the globe. This was one of my zones of genius.

I also had the space and time to explore new directions for the firm, including expanding our investment scope to include companies in the consumer supply chain. Rather than carrying out the execution myself, I entrusted our COO, Kathryn Cicoletti, to lead the execution. By the time I returned, she had already engaged a consulting firm and developed strategic options, and over the next year, her work led to the hiring of a new partner, Eric Desai, who now spearheads this investment strategy for the firm.

It was humbling to see where I wasn't needed, a lesson that offered valuable insight. This experience allowed me to focus on my best and highest use—my "zone of genius"—and to spend more time there and less time in areas where others in the firm could find and step into their zones of genius. I learned that not only is there freedom when you remove yourself from certain situations, processes, or systems but also sometimes, you get even better results.

Through this experience, I saw the profound impact of shared freedom. I realized that stepping back not only recharged me but also empowered the team to step forward and excel independently. GroundForce had become a more dynamic, capable firm, and I discovered that shared freedom was not just a personal goal; it was a strategic advantage that strengthened our organization.

Inspired by the impact of my time away, we decided to make sabbaticals an institutional practice. After five years with the firm, every team member is eligible for a monthlong sabbatical—a chance to step back, reflect, and recharge. We wanted freedom to be a core value across GroundForce, not just something for the partners. Dan took his working sabbatical the year after mine, and once again, we had the chance to grow as a firm. The team experienced my leadership style in Dan's absence, and new team members like George, Graham, and Kelly stepped up to play more active roles in his portfolio companies.

Through all of this, we experienced a distinction that research has confirmed: Not only are sabbaticals essential to recharge and refocus, but they go far beyond the benefits of a vacation. As part of his work as the founder of The Sabbatical Project, Senior Lecturer of Business Administration at Harvard University DJ DiDonna found through comprehensive interviews that sabbaticals were far more effective and impactful than vacations in combating stress, burnout, and other workplace maladies: Nearly all of them expressed how taking a prolonged period of time off helped them reenter their jobs with new vigor and perspective—or inspired them to change the direction of their work entirely. "Even though people did not go in with the same game plan," DiDonna says, "it was amazing how similar these experiences were."[16]

It was a true epiphany. By taking the risk and holding firm to what I wanted, what I needed for my own freedom, I helped create the conditions where others could do the same. In that way, we all have the chance to play to our strengths, share our gifts, and leverage each other to get the best for ourselves and the firm.

---

16 Michael Blanding, "When a Vacation Isn't Enough, a Sabbatical Can Recharge Your Life—and Your Career," Harvard Business School, February 14, 2023, https://www.library.hbs.edu/working-knowledge/when-a-vacation-isnt-enough-a-sabbatical-can-recharge-your-life-and-your-career.

The Legacy of Shared Freedom

Sharing freedom is a delicate proposition. Much of this book has focused on breaking free from external pressures—mainly that of others—which is a challenging and lifelong pursuit. For many, deepening their personal freedom and breaking free of the unconscious influences of others is hard enough and is enough—and that's valid.

But if you are open, are willing, and have a partner or team ready to play by the same rules, consider embracing *shared freedom*. It has taken years of work for Dan and me to build the trust and respect to pursue shared freedom while also prioritizing our individual freedom. We've learned to open up, be vulnerable, and trust each other. To hold space for honest feedback without reacting defensively, and if we do react, to see it as just another opportunity to learn. We can have brutally honest conversations that don't have to go perfectly, because we have done so much work together and built such a solid foundation of trust.

True shared freedom isn't about compromising your values or needs; it's about holding on to your integrity while allowing others to do the same and exploring what you can cocreate together. It's not easy, but the rewards can be extraordinary. A strong partnership or team complements strengths, protects blind spots, and offers encouragement, challenges, and perspective. It can save you from dead ends, wasted time, and unnecessary mistakes.

True partnerships require trust, vulnerability, and the courage to lean in. It's a lot like mountain climbing with a partner. Sometimes, Dan and I summit together, cheering each other on as we tackle the same peak. Other times, we're each chasing different goals, scaling separate cliffs. But what makes it work is the shared base camp we've built—a place of trust, support, and honest communication where we can regroup, rest, and plan our next climbs. Sure, there are moments when someone slips or gets tangled in their own rope. We also inevitably disappoint each other (and ourselves). That is the nature of any close relationship. We've learned to laugh, lend a hand, and keep climbing. After all, there are some peaks you cannot reach alone, and the view is always better when you have someone to share it with.

Expanding the Circle

Now that Dan and I have solidified our personal freedoms and aligned around our shared freedom, we're beginning to expand this concept to the GroundForce team and our portfolio companies. Through coaching, learning exercises, and open dialogue, we're challenging entrenched norms—like avoiding emotions or deferring to authority—encouraging the team to engage with honesty and openness.

We both believe that shared freedom broadens the definition of success. It fosters creativity, constructive critique, and collaboration. When people feel free to express themselves without fear of judgment, they contribute more authentically, driving outcomes that surpass individual ambitions.

This culture of shared freedom inspires accountability. When people feel safe to own their decisions, including their mistakes, it builds integrity and trust. Courage becomes a celebrated value, strengthening both personal and team growth. We're all learning together.

As an example, during a recent year-end performance review, Kelly, a second-year associate and one of the most junior members of our team asked, "Mark, are you available for a clearing?"

I paused, checked in with myself, and said yes.

She started, "I love your creativity and energy, and your strategic insights are great. But sometimes, you get stuck in the weeds. You'd be even more powerful to us if you set the direction and trusted us to handle the details. We'll check in; you can trust us."

Wisdom can come from anyone, as long as we're willing to hear it.

How right she was—and how incredible to get that kind of honest, thoughtful feedback. It hit one of my blind spots, and the fact that she felt comfortable enough to share it says everything about the culture we've built.

I am so grateful to have a team of sharp, talented people who not only help me see what I might miss but also have the courage to point it out—even when I don't always want to hear it.

Let me make one thing clear: Dan and I aren't doing this work because we're nice guys. We are, but that's not the reason. We both believe that this work is delivering and will continue to deliver better results for the firm and all of us, faster and easier than anything else we could do. We see it as a way to become even more successful, make an even bigger impact, and make even more money for ourselves, our team, our investors, and our companies. That is what we both want. We know it's a test. We'll know soon enough (and let you know) how it works.

Freedom doesn't have to be a solitary pursuit—it can be a shared adventure. When you surround yourself with people who share your vision and support, challenge, and encourage each other, you can build something extraordinary. True freedom isn't just personal; it inspires others by showing what's possible. At Ground-Force, we aim to deliver excellent financial results for ourselves, our companies, and our investors—not by sacrificing well-being but by creating an environment where we all can learn, earn, contribute, and grow freely.

FREEDOM TOOL: Win for All

In an environment of shared freedom, true success stems from addressing the core needs and desires of everyone involved. By taking the time to understand, express, and align these wants, needs, fears, and dreams, you can create outcomes that honor each person's goals while fostering collective growth. Use the following questions to explore how you can achieve a win for all, turning individual needs into shared opportunities for freedom.

Step 1: Clarify Core Needs

1. Identify your own core need or desire.

What is most important to you in this situation and why? How does this align with your broader goals or values?

2. Understand the other person's core need or desire.

What do they deeply want or need, and why is it meaningful to them? What is the "need behind the need"—the deeper desire they hold?

Step 2: Express Fully

1. Acknowledge your emotions.

What feelings are coming up around your needs or theirs (e.g., frustration, joy, fear)? Allow yourself to fully experience these emotions, whether by breathing deeply, moving, or vocalizing as a release.

2. Examine any stories or judgments.

What beliefs or assumptions do you have about your needs or theirs? Notice if these judgments are influencing your view, and be open to the possibility that the opposite of your perspective might also hold truth.

3. Reveal honestly.

Are there thoughts or feelings you're withholding out of fear? Consider sharing them openly with the others involved, creating space for mutual understanding.

Step 3: Appreciate and Reframe

1. Consider their needs with appreciation.

What can you value about the other party's needs, even if they differ from your own?

2. Reframe your approach with curiosity.

How else could your needs be met, beyond your initial plan? Explore alternative actions that may fulfill your goals while also honoring the other person's needs.

Step 4: Support a Win for All

1. Explore mutual support.

How could you actively help the other person meet their needs or wants? Likewise, consider ways they could support yours, creating a foundation for shared success.

By engaging with these questions, you can shift from a mindset of individual gain or win–lose to one of win–win or even win for all, including others in the organization or outside. Shared freedom means recognizing that our highest success often lies in empowering others alongside ourselves. In doing so, you foster an environment of growth, respect, and mutual support that allows everyone to thrive.

THE TAKEAWAYS
Step 7: Shared Freedom

What's the Point?

True freedom doesn't mean doing everything alone. Shared freedom allows you to lean on others without losing yourself—and often helps you go further than you could on your own.

Why Is This Important?

Great partnerships and teams don't just happen; they're built through intentional communication, shared values, trial and error, and mutual respect. Vulnerability strengthens connections, and honest feedback fuels growth.

How To: Build Shared Freedom

- **Communicate clearly and often:** Use tools like "clearing" to resolve tensions, uncover blind spots, and build trust over time.

- **Embrace vulnerability:** Open up about fears, struggles, and doubts. Real connection starts when we're willing to be real.

- **Share responsibility and empower others:** Trust your team to own their roles, make decisions, and keep you focused on your strengths.

Go Deeper

- **Books:**

  - *The 15 Commitments of Conscious Leadership* by Jim Dethmer, Diana Chapman, and Kaley Warner Klemp
  - *Radical Candor* by Kim Scott

- **Tools (markrampolla.co):**

  - Radical Clearing
  - Become a Feedback Junky
  - Clear Agreements

What's Next?

Now that you've explored the power of shared freedom, you're done! Well . . . not really. In fact, never. Freedom is an ongoing journey. Let's see if I can make sense of this all in a way that helps propel you forward, toward feeling freer in all you do and also getting more of what you want.

JOURNEY TO FREEDOM BEYOND LIMITS

Entrepreneurship is an extraordinary journey—a chance to build something unique, make an impact on the world, create wealth in all it's forms, and live on your own terms. The excitement and energy along the way are undeniable: a vivid vision, the hills and valleys, and the thrill of creating something from nothing. Entrepreneurship is all that and more, but it certainly is no guarantee of freedom. If anything, it is one of the easiest ways to get trapped by the myth of success. Too many of us buy into the idea that building a business, achieving success, and amassing wealth will set us free. This pursuit is loaded with so many "shoulds" and "shouldn'ts," comparisons, and expectations that at times it seems impossible to truly be free.

If knowing this, seeing this reality, you are still called to entrepreneurship, then go for it, but do so freely. Check in to see if you are bound by this myth or anyone else's idea of success. Define your own, and let it evolve as you grow. If you're already on the entrepreneurial path, check in with yourself. Are you doing so freely? Can you give yourself permission to take a break, pivot, or even completely change course? And if you've "made it," be cautious: Freedom may be more elusive than it appears.

Freedom takes self-awareness and discipline, but it also takes letting go of the ideal of perfection and, instead, aiming to be the best version of yourself—flaws and all. Show up as your true self, not the person you think you should be. Take the pressure off. Laugh at your humanity: *Oh, there I go again, being human!* Real freedom comes from realizing that, on the cosmic scale, nothing you do or don't do really matters. That's liberating. It frees you to act authentically, without the weight of expectations, to let go of what no longer serves you and go after whatever you want with abandonment. Freeing yourself from the perfection trap not only liberates you but also gives those around you permission to be human too. Mistakes are inevitable for all of us; embrace them as part of the process. Observe, test, learn, and come back to your own path. Freedom lies in navigating the middle ground—grounded in reality but open to endless possibilities.

Once you are well grounded in your own freedom, it's possible, beautiful, and can be beneficial to share freedom with another or many others who are also prioritizing their own freedom. If you can manage the inevitable tension between individual and shared freedom, it's incredible what can happen—a shared experience that amplifies creativity, joy, growth, and impact and creates wealth and abundance for all.

In a world of constant disruption—whether through war, economic instability, or accelerating technologies like AI—freedom becomes your anchor. When freedom is your foundation, you can adapt with clarity, navigate uncertainty with resilience, and build a life and business that's truly future proof. The greatest freedom is to think what and how you want, despite all the pressures and influences that the world and technology can throw at you.

Starting with freedom first—and returning to it always—isn't just a feel-good philosophy; it's a strategic advantage. It's the best way to get more of what you want, sooner, and it significantly increases the odds of achieving the big outcomes you dream of.

Freedom isn't somewhere out there. It's not something you have to wait for or earn. It is your birthright. It's already inside of you, right here, right now, waiting for you to claim it. It has always been that way and always will. It's available in every moment, every situation, every experience, every choice.

Just for a moment, imagine you had no limits. What if you could break away from everything that is holding you back, including gravity? What would you choose? Where would you fly? What if it were as simple as just choosing to be you?

Anthropologist Angeles Arrien shares a story told in different ways across many cultures: A wise, respected woman arrived at Heaven's gate, certain her good, productive life had earned her a place there. But the angel's only question was, "Zusai, why weren't you Zusai?"[17] This captures the essence of freedom: simply being you.

If you were completely free, what would you do right now? Do that, stay present, observe, learn, and let your journey to freedom begin.

---

17 Angeles Arrien, *The Four-Fold Way: Walking the Paths of the Warrior, Teacher, Healer, and Visionary* (HarperOne, 1993).

FROM ASHES,
EVEN GREATER FREEDOM

Little did I know how thoroughly my own freedom would be tested.

On January 7, 2025, my house, like more than six thousand others that week, was destroyed by the Pacific Palisades fire. I lost every material possession except for the clothes on my back.

In many ways, that house represented the physical manifestation of my new dream of freedom. After Maura and I separated at the end of 2020, I moved several times, exploring different LA communities to find where I felt most at home. Eventually, I fell in love with the Pacific Palisades, specifically, a 1949 mid-century modern sanctuary I discovered there. To me, the Palisades offered the perfect balance: tranquility with access to the beach, the untamed beauty of the Santa Monica Mountains, and all that LA has to offer. The day I moved into the house felt like the culmination of years of striving—a place where I could exhale, ground myself, recharge, and chart the next phase of my life.

Each morning, I stepped outside and listened to the parakeets squawking their way into the tall eucalyptus trees behind the house. Their chaotic melody, oddly soothing, transported me back to my years in Central America. At night, the calls of owls and coyotes echoed through the canyons, a symphony blending peace with wildness. The house felt alive, perfectly attuned to the rhythm of the hills.

Moving twenty times across five countries and seven states had taught me how to settle in quickly, but this time, I took a different approach. I gave myself a full year to create something truly special. Even though I was renting, I invested what some might call a ridiculous amount of money. But for me, it was worth it. For the first time in over twenty-five years, I was creating a space that was entirely mine—designed exactly the way I wanted.

The result? A home that felt both zen and alive.

Succulents and towering palms filled the rooms, blending with cherished artwork and curiosities from around the world. A custom-built twenty-person dining table stood proudly on the deck. From there, the Pacific Ocean stretched endlessly, with Catalina Island faintly visible on the horizon—a view that never ceased to remind me how far I had come. I installed an eight-person barrel sauna and cold plunge, sculptures, blackout curtains, a high-end sound system, and more.

The family room became my favorite space. Refurbished Knoll couches from the Long Beach Antique Market paired perfectly with a gorgeous rug and wooden coffee tables from El Salvador. Of course, more plants filled the room. Every detail was intentional. Even my closet—a marvel of organization—was a small point of pride. I could almost hear my brother John teasing me about my childhood messiness, but this space reflected the freedom I'd found in order and self-awareness.

Over the prior year, I had fallen in love with Caroline, a wonderful and beautiful Brit. She visited often and loved the house as much as I did. She affectionately nicknamed it "Goucher," after the street it was on, and brought her impeccable design aesthetic and savvy negotiation skills to enhance every detail. She commissioned custom outdoor furniture, stocked the kitchen with chef-grade essentials, adorned each room with elegant linens, and created a painting I adored, which became the dining room's centerpiece. Together, we reveled in the home's energy, breathtaking views, and the peace and joy we so beautifully cocreated.

As much as I love community, I know myself: I'm a lone wolf at heart, and living alone in Goucher suited me perfectly. But I loved it when the house came alive with visitors. My sister stayed in the pool house for months, transforming it into her own wellness retreat while she focused on healing. My lifelong friend Stew worked poolside during football season while his son practiced at Pali High. Family and friends came and went—my sister Karen for a week, Sara and her mom, Sajma, from our extended Bosnian family, and finally my daughters and cousin Brigid over the holidays, filling the house with laughter, life, and love. Caroline and I hosted numerous dinners with friends and business associates, planning even more for 2025.

The energy reached another level when Caroline's kids visited. Her daughter Siva's birthday party with thirteen other eleven-year-olds was a joyful riot, while her son Rumi and his friends staged slam-dunk competitions in the pool basketball hoop. I loved their chaos.

The house was minutes from the beach, so I could still stand-up paddle surf and outrigger. But over the years, I had realized that, as much as I loved our house in Redondo, I loved the hills even more than the beach. The Santa Monica Mountains became my playground. After years of back pain, I was finally strong enough to bike those hills again. Just two days before the fires, I cruised twenty miles along the fire roads on my e-bike, feeling invincible—completely oblivious that soon, the entire state park would look like the set of a postapocalyptic movie.

In that house, I tested and refined my personal routines, creating a rhythm that served me well and allowed my time there to become the most professionally productive of my life. Mornings began with workouts, followed by meditation, sauna, and a cold plunge—rituals that left me focused and energized. My home office, a beautiful and serene space, became the perfect environment for deep work on Mondays and Fridays.

Evenings were a mix of simplicity and ritual. Some nights, I cooked; other times, I treated myself to the Erewhon food bar down the hill—where the meals were five-star quality and priced to match. I usually paired my meals with a Partake nonalcoholic beer or a mocktail in one of my nice wine glasses. In this house, I had wrestled my overindulgent demons to the ground—or perhaps embraced them in a warm, loving hug.

At night, I'd draw the blackout curtains, soak in a warm bath, and read as the calls of my wildlife friends echoed through the hills. Those moments reminded me how this house had become a reflection of my freedom—a space deliberately built, detail by detail, to align with the life I wanted.

And then it was gone.

In the days and weeks after the fire, I found myself leaning heavily on the principles I've written about in this book. The irony wasn't lost on me: I was now being tested in the most personal and profound way. So I chose to follow my own advice.

I know myself well now. I thrive in a crisis, easily powering through, for a time, with focus, determination, and compassion for others—but often neglecting that same care for myself.

To resist that pattern, I remade a list I'd kept in my home office:

What am I avoiding, suppressing, ignoring, denying, minimizing, or rationalizing? This time, I refused to rush into solving or diving into finding another house to escape discomfort. Instead, I asked, *How can I stay fully present and learn everything there is to learn from this experience?*

I gave myself permission to feel everything. For the first few days, I was in and out of shock, especially when Caroline and I ventured through the devastation in tears to see what was left of our beloved Goucher. Then came grief—the deep sadness of losing a home that symbolized years of intentionality: all the beautiful memories, photos, books, and mementos. Anger followed: at local leaders, nature, the world—and at myself for deciding to go "self-insured" the year before. Guilt crept in too: I had the resources to recover while so many others did not. I also felt sparks of excitement: What if this was a chance to dream again? To create something new and even more amazing?

Some days, I cycled through every emotion in a single hour, but I leaned into the practices I teach, running through the Freedom Key until I felt like I'd built an emotional processing supercomputer. I wasn't unaffected; I had simply gotten so good at processing my emotions that it seemed I could face anything, sometimes in seconds, sometimes over days, but always fully. I felt imperturbable because I was willing and able to experience it all.

Life didn't stop. It never does for entrepreneurs. Even amid loss and upheaval, there were meetings, decisions, and deadlines. Companies needed guidance, investment opportunities popped up, and emails multiplied like rabbits. But this time, I took a more measured approach: rational hours, clear priorities, and delegation. No heroics. If a meeting was important or gave me an "energy up," I showed up fully. If not, I sent it to the graveyard of postponed Zoom calls—may they rest in peace.

Of course, I also had to "get shit done." So I dove into solve mode at times: cancel bills, find a new place, buy underwear. Some days, I felt unstoppable; others, it was a struggle to write a few emails.

At times, I felt alone, as I had in ZICO's early days. But this time, I did something different: I opened up. I talked openly with family, friends, and my team at GroundForce about my feelings and struggles. I wrote about my experience, did interviews, helped others where I could, and allowed others to help me. Caroline and I "cleared" emotions together multiple times a day as we navigated the chaos, including her and her kids having to evacuate her house and the four of us staying in three different hotels and a house in Santa Barbara, generously lent to us by a friend of a friend over the first three weeks post-fires. The stress tested us—but it also brought us closer.

Living out of hotels and Airbnbs for weeks felt like an extended game of Where's My Charger? My routines? Gone. Instead, I had to get creative: cramming workouts into closet-sized spaces, meditating through the sound of sirens as fire crews still raced toward emergencies, writing on whatever flat surface I could find, and resisting the endless pull of late-night news feeds. Bit by bit, I pieced together a version of stability—more DIY than designer, but it worked.

Amid the challenges, that early spark of excitement grew: *Could this loss reveal ways I still wasn't as free as I thought? How could this be the best thing for me? What if the fire didn't happen to* me *but for* me? *Could it be a chance to realign with what I truly want—to shed what no longer serves me and step into a new chapter of freedom with even more success, wealth, meaning, and deeper relationships?*

In the face of such loss, I found myself not broken but liberated. Stripped of the markers of success—a beautiful house and all it contained—I discovered that the essence of my life was intact, perhaps more potent than ever. The fire took everything tangible but left me with an undeniable truth: Freedom isn't what you own; it's what you carry within you.

That realization stirred immense gratitude. Gratitude for the memories and the opportunity to live in that amazing house. Gratitude for the incredible people I had met over the years and relationships I had built. Gratitude for the clarity this loss brought—that freedom isn't tied to a place any more than it is to wealth or success. Gratitude for the amazing life I had lived thus far and for the incredible opportunities ahead for me.

This book was meant to guide others, but in those raw, uncertain days, it also guided me. It reminded me that freedom isn't a fixed destination; it's a practice. It deepened my understanding of what freedom requires: the courage to see reality as it is, to know and celebrate myself; the courage to break free of what is holding me back; the audacity to dream again—even from ashes; discipline; the willingness and ability to change; and the power of cocreating with others.

Even while the hills around LA still burned, clarity and a renewed sense of purpose emerged. I became clearer than ever about what I wanted: More success. More wealth, in all it's forms. More meaning. But also more connection, more life, more love. I still wanted it all—maybe even more than ever—but I now knew freedom must come first. Freedom isn't something I would chase or claim at the finish line; it would be my foundation, a choice I would do my best to make at every moment, no matter the circumstances.

With freedom as my foundation, I am now dreaming bigger, taking bolder but calculated risks, and embracing life's possibilities. The fire stripped away the illusions of what I thought I needed, leaving only what truly matters to me. So I surrender to the unknown, rebuild with intention, and trust in what will rise from the ashes. Whatever comes next, I am ready. I am free.

ACKNOWLEDGMENTS

Lao Tzu, the great Chinese philosopher and founder of Taoism, said that he did not teach the truth. He didn't believe such a thing existed. Instead, he pointed to what we already know but have forgotten. I know the wisdom of these words. Throughout the process of writing this book, I often felt like a flawed channel—less an originator of ideas and more a conduit for something larger than myself. At times, the best I could do was step aside, quiet my mind, and allow whatever wanted to come through to do so. The full list of those who have influenced this book would stretch beyond these pages, but I want to recognize a few near-in teachers with my deepest gratitude.

My beautiful and magical partner, Caroline Gamble—your love, wisdom, and unwavering belief in me have been both a sanctuary and a spark. You inspired, challenged, and soothed me through the birth of this manuscript, and I feel endlessly grateful to walk this path with you, as you suggested, choosing daily and choosing wisely.

To my wonderful daughters, Ciara and Lexi—you are my greatest inspiration. Your love, honesty, and even your brutally loving feedback have shaped not just this book but my life. Maura, thank you for the feedback on this book. I am forever grateful for the years we shared, the family we built, and the way we have navigated a new chapter with mutual love and respect.

To Mary Beth—our time together in Pacific Palisades was brief but extraordinary, and your wisdom and encouragement around all my choices, including this book, have meant the world.

To Brigid Connery—my third daughter by fate—who just happened to be in the Palisades and gave me brutal but necessary feedback on an early draft. Thank you!

To the team at GroundForce Capital—you have helped me refine these ideas in action, allowing me to find (and mostly stay in) my zone of genius as we continue building one of the best firms in finance. A special thanks to my partner, Dan Gluck, one of the most important relationships of my life, for allowing me to be fully myself, while challenging, supporting, and celebrating me in all the right ways—including on this book. To Kathryn Cicoletti and Sarah Robson, for your invaluable feedback, support, and encouragement. And to Nicola D'Alton, for keeping me (as close to) organized and on track as possible and for being a willing participant in applying some of the tools and philosophy of this book while still quite raw.

To the extraordinary personal development team I have had around me—Agnes Regeczkey, Kat Agostino, Deb Katz, and Jim Fallon—your insights and wisdom have helped shape both this book and my life.

To The Conscious Leadership Group—your training, tools, and coaching have transformed how I lead and live, and have deeply influenced so much of this book.

To the early readers—Andre Matin, Marcus Bell, Elizabeth Angel, JR Smich, and Josh Church—your input and feedback refined and sharpened my words in the best possible ways.

To the teams at Greenleaf and Inc. Magazine—Justin Branch, Benito Salazar, Erin Brown, Hayden Seder, Trinity Massengale, and so many more—your belief in me and this project humbled me and gave me confidence when I needed it most.

The teams of all the portfolio companies at PowerPlant and GroundForce—I have learned so much from each of you, and it is an honor to support you on your journey. Special thanks to the team at ZICO Rising, both US and Thailand—your discipline, dedication, and drive have taken a brand I love and carried it further than I ever could alone, giving me the freedom to focus on so much more, including this book.

Our investors, operating advisors, and the many supporters of PowerPlant and GroundForce Capital—I deeply appreciate your trust, support, and partnership.

My friends in life and business—those who have taught me, challenged me, and walked this path alongside me—you continue to shape my understanding of business, leadership, and life.

And finally, all the entrepreneurs out there—you are my greatest teachers. You inspire and motivate me every day. If I can play even a small role in your journey, I am honored to do so.

—Mark Rampolla,
March 2025, Los Angeles

ABOUT THE AUTHOR

MARK RAMPOLLA is a visionary entrepreneur, investor, writer, speaker, and coach, known for inspiring mission-driven leaders to build businesses that matter. As co-founder and comanaging partner of GroundForce Capital, he guides bold founders to scale companies with purpose and impact.

Previously, Mark founded ZICO Coconut Water, pioneering the multibillion-dollar coconut water category and selling the brand to The Coca-Cola Company—before famously buying it back.

Over his career, Mark has invested in more than one hundred companies, served on over twenty boards, raised more than $1 billion in capital, and created over $5 billion in enterprise value and tens of thousands of jobs. His influence has shaped industries, accelerated movements, and empowered a generation of conscious entrepreneurs.

A former Peace Corps volunteer, corporate executive, and author of *High-Hanging Fruit*, Mark is deeply passionate about helping entrepreneurs break free—from mental, emotional, financial, and societal constraints—to live and lead with true freedom. He graduated from Marquette University with his BA in business, and holds an MBA and Master's of Environmental Management from Duke University.

Since losing his home in the 2025 Pacific Palisades fires, Mark has been wandering. But not every wanderer is lost.

For more about Mark, visit MarkRampolla.co